Parenting Inspired

Finding Grace in the Chaos, Confidence in Yourself, and Gentle Joy along the Way

A self-coaching model for parents seeking to create positive change in their families

Alice Hanscam
PCI Certified Parent Coach®

ISBN: 1502804484

ISBN 13: 9781502804488

Library of Congress Control Number: 2014918456

CreateSpace Independent Publishing Platform

North Charleston, South Carolina

A few words from others...

"As parents, Alice has gently set us on the relationship path we envision for our family, helped us realize we are not alone in our day-to-day struggles and provided the simplest of tools that will last throughout our parenting journey. With her guidance, what used to be explosive situations are defusing much more quickly and everyday battles are evolving into calm, even fun routines. *Parenting Inspired* has helped us learn how to move more smoothly through the chaos and be the calming presence our child needs as he navigates huge emotions and experiences life changes."

— Theresa Buckley Perez, parent

"The challenge of being a parent is the job doesn't come with a manual. Something happens, and in the minute when we have to respond to our child's behavior we respond from our gut. Many times what comes out of our mouths leaves us feeling like inept and even bad parents. Yet we can't figure out what else to do or say. *Parenting Inspired* is the answer. Alice Hanscam's new book helps parents move from "What should I do?" to "I know what I want to have happen" and make it a reality. It's a readable, doable framework from which you can grow into the parent you always wanted to be and have the relationship with your children that you always dreamed about."

— Rhonda Moskowitz, M.A., PCI Certified Parent Coach®, founder of Practical Solutions Parent Coaching

"Alice speaks from her big heart, both as a mother and as a parent coach. She expertly takes parents on a reflective journey through the phases of Appreciative Inquiry while sharing real-life stories of her own and of her clients. Readers experience first-hand the positive results of her compassionate caring and wise techniques. Inspired parenting, indeed!"

— Gloria DeGaetano, founder, The Parent Coaching Institute

Dedication

To all parents striving to find the grace, confidence, and joy in their relationships with their children—to thrive as a family!

Contents

Foreword

I am a mother. I may have an extensive background in all things children, but first and foremost I am a mother. Like you, I have been over-the-top exhausted and filled with pride and joy. I've wept at length, raged, laughed, and loved all in the name of parenting. I've been frustrated as yet again I woke to my baby's hourly cries, wondering how I would make it through the next day. I've wept on the preschool teacher's shoulder as I tried to understand how my sweet little girl could become such a feisty, fight-me-at-every-step-of-the-way four-year-old. I've felt the heat climb in me as my child pushed my buttons for the umpteenth time that day. I've felt my heart break as my daughters' friends were unkind or downright mean and felt confused about how best to help them through this deep sadness—or even if I could or should. I've struggled with just how much homework help to give, especially as my child sat at the table in tears over the work in front of her, certain she was a failure. I've been frightened when my husband and I lost contact at length with our teens during a touch-and-go winter drive that left them stuck in the snowy mountains far from home. I've yelled in an effort to "get them to listen," or to make sure I had the last word (that never worked). I've also felt the pride and joy as they accomplished amazing things and were happy and excited about life, school, and friends. And I've grown through it all, enriching my relationships with my children, my spouse, even myself in ways I never dreamed of, exercising muscles I never knew I had, becoming a better person and parent along the way.

My sincere desire is for you to grow as well. To grow with intention to be the kind of parent you wish to be and have the kind of relationships with your children you truly want. To parent with gentle joy, and be able to welcome all that your parenting journey may bring. To experience the greater ease, confidence, and deep satisfaction that awaits you as you focus on your own growth. What a gift this can be to your children, to your family, and to you. I invite you to join me, a parent coach *and* a mother, and to feel encouraged, supported, and empowered. Parenting is, by far, the most difficult, the most reward-ing, the most important job we have. Let's do it well.

This book was written to guide you step by step through the pro-cess of an inspired parenting journey. For this reason, it is meant to be read and digested slowly, its parts considered with care. You may be tempted to skip ahead to parts that intrigue you, yet you will be better served to take this book one step at a time. Now you are more likely to create the real and lasting change you truly want. Know that this process has worked well, and continues to work well, for me and many others—it is a process you can return to often, a way of life you can embrace, and it can enrich all your relationships.

Perhaps you are coming to this book overwhelmed, exhausted, and desperately wanting things in your family to be different. It may be difficult for you to envision parenting as a rewarding, joyful jour-ney. It may be difficult for you to think you could ever feel the calm connection and confidence you truly want. And yet this can be your experience. Let this book gently guide you toward parenting inspired, finding grace in the chaos (oh, and chaos there will be!), confidence in yourself, and more joy in all that you do. I think you will delight in the journey that awaits you!

Finally, I share stories from my experience as a PCI Certified Parent Coach®. All names and identifying details have been altered to pro-tect the confidentiality of the amazing parents I've been blessed to work with. Know that the integrity of the stories has been maintained throughout. Let them encourage and inspire you along your way!

Alice

Introduction

Before we embark on our journey...

As a PCI Certified Parent Coach® I partner with parents to help them create the positive change they want in their families. It is important to share briefly the framework within which I coach and this book is written. Appreciative Inquiry[1] ("AI") was first developed by David Cooperrider[2] about thirty years ago as a positive change methodology for the corporate world. Its use has grown extensively over the years and reached into personal lives in rich and inspiring ways, guiding people—and parents like you—toward the kind of relationships and experiences they really want. Gloria DeGaetano, founder of the Parent Coaching Institute[3], is the pioneer for bringing AI to parenting. As I live and coach AI, my clients and I are blessed with more meaningful relationships and more joyful experiences—inspiring me to continue bringing this way of creating real and lasting change to as many of you as possible.

Appreciative Inquiry, or "AI," is founded on five principles:

The Constructionist Principle speaks to how we co-create our life experience as we work together, listening, seeking to understand, and sharing our stories. We are inter-connected—and this can be powerful as we parent, knowing that our thoughts, feelings, and actions can directly or indirectly influence our children and ultimately create our family experience.

The Simultaneity Principle highlights how change begins with the first questions we ask. We create more of whatever we inquire into. Let's ask ourselves about what we want more of in our lives! Perhaps we want calm connection with our children, greater confidence and joy, a more peaceful household...

The Anticipatory Principle emphasizes how the images we create of our future will guide our current behavior. What we focus on grows. Let's get clear about where we intend to head on this parenting journey, what kind of relationships we want to grow, what kind of qualities are important to us—and now we are more likely to be able to act in alignment with what we want the most, even during the chaos of tough times.

The Poetic Principle speaks to all the rich and inspiring stories we have to share and learn from. As parents, we have plenty! Sharing them can be empowering.

The Positive Principle emphasizes how the more positive the questions we ask, the more effective the change we are trying to create. A positive focus builds hope, inspiration, and joy, energizing us as we work to create the change we desire.

These five principles form the theory behind AI. The process within which we use these principles and which you will journey through in this book is called "The 4 Ds"[4]—four phases we move through as we create the change we want:

- **The Discovery phase** is the process of finding what has worked and is working for you, what your strengths are, what is going well, what you can appreciate in the midst of whatever turmoil you are finding yourself in. This is the foundation for the entire coaching process.

- **The Dream phase** has us clarifying exactly what your "preferred future" looks and feels like.

- **The Design phase** incorporates the specific steps you've identified to help you reach your "preferred future"—the change you desire. These steps are based on your strengths and what works for you.

- **The Destiny phase** is reached when you find yourself living your Dream more and more, and working on maintaining it and growing it. Time to celebrate!

In addition to the "4 Ds" there are three guiding touchstones or tools for your successful parenting journey that can influence all your relationships in positive and meaningful ways:

What You Focus on Grows...[5]

This has been the most powerful element in all my growth and in the growth of my clients. You will read these five words often in this book, and the more you take them to heart, the more they can bring you incredible gifts. Focus on what you want more of. Pay attention to when things are going well, when a strength of yours really steps up. Intentionally look for the calm, connected, confident, joyful qualities of your parenting journey. Focus more on when your children behave positively or even neutrally. As you run errands or go through a long workday, pay attention to the little things you can appreciate. *What you focus on grows*—this book is really all about shifting your focus in order to grow the kind of relationships and parenting experience you want the most. It works. It is contagious. "What you focus on grows" is a muscle to exercise every day.

The Power of Pause...[6]

This is your number-one tool on your tool belt of life. It can benefit every relationship you have, including your relationship with yourself, and it's really quite simple. Pausing came to my attention through one of the most inspiring parenting books I've read—*ScreamFree Parenting* by Hal Runkel.

Take a moment and consider when you have felt really good about how you behaved in a conflict or heated moment.

What did you notice about yourself?

Most parents notice they felt calm, clear, connected, matter-of-fact, (reasonably) comfortable…or some combination of these. And many will say that the heated moment became a nonissue, or at least a much less intense one, and they felt good about the outcome. What works for you to find that place of calm in the midst of conflict? What do you realize you do that lets your calm(er) self lead the way? *This is the moment we pause.* Pausing gives us the brief second, minutes, or hours we need to take care of our own upset feelings, to calm down, to think about what we really want in the situation. We can then re-enter a situation and respond to it based on what we really want (to encourage our preschooler to share, for instance) rather than reacting to the emotions or circumstance of the moment (yelling at them to give their toy up NOW…) This can build relationships in positive and respectful ways, for now we are communicating that our child can count on us to keep it together no matter what they do—what a way to build trust; we are communicating respect by being more respectful ourselves. We tend to listen better, interact more gently, and more likely guide our child toward just what we want to see more of (sharing in the future?). *Truly relationship building.*

Pausing can take many forms. A few that can work well for parents include:

- **Counting to ten**
- **Taking a few deep breaths**
- **Breaking eye contact**

- **Focusing on another task**
- **Walking away**
- **Encouraging self-talk**
- **Sitting next to your child**
- **Closing your eyes**
- **Getting a drink of water**
- **Putting a piece of furniture between you and your child**
- **Saying, "Let me think about it and I will get back to you..."**

Focus on what works for you to pause. Learn to recognize when you are heating up and what can help you stop, calm down, think—and then respond instead of react. Reflect on the times you felt good about how you behaved in a conflict or challenge, on the moment you could feel the heat rising in you, and what you did to not let your anger or frustration take over—what you did that left you feeling calmer and able to respond instead of react.

What worked for me was breaking eye contact and focusing on cleaning the kitchen counter. This often created the pause I needed—I'd let my anger carry me off to the kitchen, I'd swipe at the counter, give my adrenaline an outlet, and whew, I'd feel better, calmer, able to think. A parent I coached discovered that what worked for her to pause was walking away to get a drink of water, giving her a moment to breathe and think. I do believe that some days she felt she was drowning with all the water pauses she took! With toddlers who often need you to stay near, briefly closing your eyes or intentionally taking a few deep breaths as you, for instance, gently stop them from hitting can create the pause needed to find that place of calm (and stay gentle!). With our teens, we can say, "I hear you. I need to think about it. I will get back to you." Then be sure to follow through and get back to them! As you grow this ability, notice how it influences situations and your children, how you end up feeling, what is different for you.

Exercise your Pause muscle!

Like a muscle, pausing gets stronger with use. One way that helped me stay focused on pausing was sticking notes with the word "pause" written on them in areas I frequented—the microwave, in my car, on my bathroom mirror.

Another parent I worked with drew a pause button on her hand—and engaged her children in pushing it when she needed it the most. That brought laughter—another excellent parenting tool—into the mix, lightening up potentially heated moments.

Find what works for you to keep The Power of Pause at the fore-front of your brain. Then watch as life calms down, relationships feel better, and your confidence in all you do grows. How cool is that?

Self-care...

Taking care of you is the foundation for parenting and living well.[7] What have you done today, just for you? What would you like to do? Self-care comes in many packages—lengthy workouts, walking your dog, drinking a cup of tea, taking a few deep breaths, moving forward with a project, running errands by yourself, pausing to gaze at the beautiful sunset. You have good company if you feel like there is no time for you—what with work, chores, kids to pick up and drop off, dinner to make, laundry to do, diapers to change, a bathroom to clean, e-mails to answer, errands to run—really, where IS the time? Yet taking even a few minutes just for you each day or a few hours a week can make parenting and the chaos that comes with it a little bit easier.

Your self-care savings account

Consider your self-care a savings account—envision
it as separate from you, something you deposit into
daily. Each thing you do intentionally and just for you
becomes a deposit that you now can draw from in
challenging times. It can be a large deposit—like a
workout at a gym or a date with your spouse, or small—
stepping outdoors to breathe deeply, making a cup
of tea. No matter the size, they all count and add up.
And when the going gets tough you now have a solid
account to withdraw from, rather than withdrawing
directly from yourself. This gave me the added energy
and patience that was so often needed each
day, and I believe it can for you as well.

You will discover how the things you've done just for
you even a few days ago can support you today, in
the heat of the moment, by just knowing you've done
so and affirming it for yourself. Like a bank account,
deposits are there to lean on days or weeks later. Rather
like that wonderful vacation you may have had last
year, or the brisk walk from last week...just reflecting
on it can remind you of the good feelings, the refueling
it did, the rest or adventure it provided. And now it
can step up to benefit you in the chaos of today.

You can deposit, you can withdraw,
and you can feel strong either way.

With a solid self-care bank account we can be more patient, resilient, and creative. We can more likely have a sense of humor and clarity on what we want. We can let go and move on more easily. We can forgive ourselves, accept our preschooler's rather volcanic feelings, not take personally our teen's eye-rolling, go with the flow as the casserole burns and it is cereal or take-out once again for dinner. *I encourage you to bring self-care back into focus.* Discover what feels good to you and know as you do things intentionally they can make a difference. This is a key part of parenting well.

Keep *What You Focus on Grows*, *The Power of Pause* and *Self-Care* close by, exercise them often, and you are already on your way to feeling greater ease, confidence, and joy in your parenting, and in your relationships with your children!

One final note before we move on...

Parenting is less about kids and much, much more about parents. As you grow your calm and confident self, you are directly influencing your children—relationships can become more connected and joyful, life can calm down—with the "simple" step of focusing first on you and your own growth.[8] Consider asking a friend, your parenting partner, or a relative to work alongside you on this journey. Encased in a relationship with another, the power and influence of this process can be exponential.

No matter how you choose to embrace this process, savor it. Real and lasting change takes the respect of time. Relationships deserve this.

Let's get started!

Discovery

Let's Discover!

W hat has put a smile on your face this week? When have you felt especially good about how your children behaved? Where do you feel the most confident as a parent?

Discovery is the core of this entire journey you are embarking on. If you were to do any one thing on a regular basis, I encourage you to focus on just this—discovering. Reflect on all your successes— where things have gone well, where they are currently working, what strengths have truly benefitted you. Discovery is all about uncovering, remembering, and focusing on your positive history as a parent, on what—including right now, today—is working for you or can be appreciated no matter the yuck or chaos it is encased in. Maybe it is your child's quick smile in the midst of trouble that made you nearly smile as well; maybe it is your surprising patience as your child stubbornly persists at getting something "just so." Remember the positive moments from yesterday, a year ago, or today. As you discover, you will find how good doing so can feel; how fun, enlightening, and even inspiring it can be. Enjoy!

Story Time!

Listen to what others experienced in the Discovery phase

Tom and Sarah's story

Tom and Sarah were having trouble with their thirteen-year-old son, Erik. Disrespect, less than desirable school performance, and a lack of responsibility had both parents frustrated, concerned, and caught up in their buttons being pushed—reactivity was the name of the game. They came to coaching hoping to understand their son better, feel more even-keeled, and to help him be more respectful, responsible, and successful in school. As Discovery unfolded, we explored when they had felt best about how Erik behaved, as well as when they had felt good about how *they* had behaved in a heated exchange; when they were especially pleased with responsible behavior; and where they noticed he was most engaged in school and learning.

The steps they initially took—**focusing first on themselves in order to pause and calm down, and spending time intentionally noticing what their son did well** (a step you will be introduced to a bit later)—gifted moments that grew their relationship with their son in positive, healthy ways. A car ride that was preceded by an accidental car door whack on the head (via the son) and tempers that wanted to flare became a ride of quiet connection. Sarah (the one with the pounding headache) breathed (pause!), reached out and touched her son, affirmed that "accidents happen," and found herself able to stay quiet, giving him space to process his feelings and her time to feel better. Staying quiet had been a challenge for Sarah—she'd often find herself repeating and rehashing an issue, frustrated with the increasing clamming up of her teen. This time, she let her focus on pausing step up. The car ride became comfortable as a result. And Dad, seething initially in the front seat, found himself able to calm as he respectfully gave his wife the opportunity to connect with and affirm their son. Pauses all around that brought a potentially yucky situation to one with honest and heartfelt connection. And a pleasant car ride! Even the pain of the injury seemed to subside.

Noticing what their son did well ended up filling Tom and Sarah's buckets immensely! Instead of spending the week immersed in all that their son was doing wrong, they looked for the right and good. Their list at our next session was simply amazing. It included their son's athletic ability and his positive attitude toward his sport, his helpfulness that stepped up now and again, his sense of humor, and how he took care of his own laundry, stood firm in his beliefs, and really got excited about the hands-on projects his teachers assigned. Tom and Sarah reframed some of what irritates them about their son into things they could appreciate—his stubbornness became "standing firm," his lack of responsibility in many places yielded to their appreciation that he DID do his laundry AND usually put it away. They considered how positive he could be toward things he was passionate about—never mind the negative, disgruntled behavior in other areas. It even caught them by surprise to notice just where their son did do well in school—when he could work with others, moving, discussing, and creating.

As a result of their work in Discovery, they began to be gifted with moments that meant a great deal to them. A situation at a football practice of Erik's had Tom initially irritated, then focusing on ***pause*** as he headed across the field to talk with his son, thinking about how he wanted the situation to look and feel, and calming down. By the time he reached Erik to address the issue, Tom interacted with calm connection. The gift in this? What his son said. "Wow, Dad. You've changed. You used to let these things get you mad!" For Tom, it was like a light bulb went off. His effort at calming himself and creating connection was noticed and appreciated by Erik. Knowing he was role modeling exactly what he wanted more of left Tom feeling encouraged and committed to keep exercising his pause muscle, to keep calm connection his goal. It felt *good.*

When Erik was given the okay to bike to a friend's one evening, with the expectation that he was to be home before dark, another gift emerged. Erik lost track of time and called for a pick up via Mom. This pushed Sarah's button—"I told him to be home, why couldn't he pay attention, I have better things to do then pick him up," were the thoughts running through her head. Sarah let our coaching guide her as she used her drive to pause—to breathe, calm herself, and reflect on what she really wanted to communicate to Erik—rather than just blow up at him for being irresponsible. She found herself appreciating his ability to call and ask for a ride, even though he knew she'd be upset with him. She thought about his growing independence and how she wanted to support that. Lucky Erik, for by the time Mom showed up she was calm and collected—at least on the outside. Sarah listened to Erik's story of why he lost track of time, asked him what he could do differently next time (communicating her confidence in his abilities—empowering for a child!), and let go of wanting to berate him for making the mistake and dragging her out late at night. This was tough for Sarah, and seeking Tom out privately to unload her frustrations allowed her to continue staying in her pause mode. Teamwork!

The next day brought a second chance for Erik to step up and take responsibility—Sarah was able to let him head off once again on his bike without saying a word, communicating her confidence in and respect for the plan he shared the night before. Her ability to let pause help her stay quiet at key moments was really growing. The ultimate gift? Erik followed through with just what he said he'd do differently... and he was home on time. Tom and Sarah were relieved and encouraged—their son showed how he could take responsibility for himself, especially when they were able to give him the respectful space to do so. And this began to ripple out to other areas of his life—school, sports, chores...Pause—it is powerful.

Mary's story

Mary was overwhelmed. Two young children, one a challenging toddler, the other a whiny, testy, sassy four-year-old, and life at a fast pace. She was tired of yelling, of kids who didn't listen, of how frustrated she got as her four-year-old melted down as the day wore on—or just as the day began and they needed to head out the door! Mary came to coaching to gain confidence and ease in her parenting; to have a calmer, more respectful household; and to feel in control of herself. With our focus on what has worked and felt good to her, we discovered times she felt proud of how she handled a conflict or challenge, when things went most smoothly and felt comfortable and at ease, and where she felt confident as a parent.

The steps Mary initially took included **focusing on self-care, pausing in order to calm herself, and noticing what put a smile on her face in regard to her children**. Mary's attention to getting time for herself resulted in Grandma stepping up to take Jake and Olivia for an overnight, and had Mary being more determined to make it to her exercise class. Intentionally taking care of herself left her feeling good—accomplished and energized. She combined this with noticing when she felt the most confident and in control, and realized that in the past when she had a consistent rhythm in place that included exercise, she felt calmer, more confident, and definitely in control of herself. These times were defined by her clarity over what she wanted to do (exercise), her kids knowing what to expect, a regular routine in place, and lots of outdoor and exercise time. The Aha moment for Mary was recognizing how having a rhythm or routine in place typically allowed their day to pleasantly unfold. Everyone felt better, calmer, more cooperative. These were the days she felt at her best!

As Mary reflected on the times she handled conflict well, she noticed that they were times when she created a pause for herself. She discovered that when she stayed calm, Jake and Olivia were more likely to be calmer and more cooperative. And her calm times had her feeling more present to her children, clearer on her expectations, patient. She shared how she'd be more likely to address potential problems or conflicts with lighthearted exchanges: "Uh oh! Your juice spilled!" "Hands to yourself, please!" "If you need to whine, the downstairs is the whining place in our house..." Her pause consisted of encouraging self-talk—she'd consider what she could appreciate about her son, what put a smile on her face, what she really wanted in a situation—and then she'd respond to his antics or whining from her newfound calm place, more easily clarifying expectations. As a result Jake more often chose to clean up the juice, use gentle hands, take a break until he was ready to use a "regular" voice. This led to more positive family times, which were truly relationship building. Pausing began to be Mary's mantra.

Taking time to notice what put a smile on her face had Mary coming back to each of our early sessions with a delightful list—Jake the Scientist moment when her son was mixing and tasting a variety of ingredients, Olivia working long and hard on putting her shoes on by herself with a final "I DID it!"—wrong feet and all, "I love you Mommy with all my heart!" spontaneously expressed—hug included, the mustard and peanut butter sandwich created and eaten, watching Jake in his first circle time at his preschool bravely raising his hand and waiting patiently for his turn to share. This led to noticing qualities in her children that she hadn't recognized before. She began to appreciate Jake's natural curiosity, his ability to wait—at least in preschool!—and how secure and comfortable he must feel to be able to share in circle time. Mary noticed how capable her toddler Olivia was when it came to dressing, and she decided shoes on the wrong feet were totally acceptable ☺. Mary found as she looked for the smile moments that she was relaxing and was more able to call on the ability to pause, be calm, go with the flow, and feel in control of herself. It really rippled out in huge ways for her. Instead of angst over two- and four-year-old antics, she found a bit more joy...mustard and peanut-butter sandwiches and all. Her work in Discovery helped her begin to truly see all that was working for her; what she did well; and how important fun family times, cooperation, and joy in parenting were to her. Mary began to relax.

Steve and Elizabeth's story

Steve and Elizabeth came to coaching to calm themselves down. Three school-aged children, fourteen-year-old Erin, eleven-year-old Leah, and six-year-old Kelly, who were busily pushing their buttons, being disrespectful, and playing one parent off of the other, had them feeling exhausted, angry, frustrated—and often resorting to punishments that no one felt good about. We spent a long time in Discovery, moving away from these negative feelings and instead finding the times Steve and Elizabeth felt truly a team as parents, especially good about how they behaved in a heated situation, and when Erin, Leah, and Kelly were most respectful, cooperative, and able to listen well. One example that stood out was whenever Elizabeth came home with the groceries—she and Steve realized how all three girls joined in to help unload (without complaining), and willingly followed through with putting the groceries away. Everyone worked together, in good spirits, cooperating with and respecting each other. Steve and Elizabeth recognized how clear the expectation was for the girls (we all help with the groceries!), how calm and matter-of-fact they felt, and how light humor and conversation highlighted these times. One of the gifts of Discovery is the good feelings that emerge as parents intentionally focus on where things are going well—and this certainly was true for Steve and Elizabeth!

Pause and self-care were key for Steve and Elizabeth. They worked hard at focusing first on themselves when they felt their buttons being pushed, and discovered how taking a break behind a closed door, doing something with their hands, taking a short walk, or folding laundry gave them the breather necessary to be more thoughtful in their response to the button pusher. Their growing ability to pause gifted them brief moments of connection and cooperation with their children that caught them by surprise. Steve found himself clearly communicating to eleven-year-old Leah what was expected from her chore-wise, and walking away when she reacted with the "You can't make me" attitude, taking a break in his bedroom and then joining his wife for a short walk. Self-care and pause at their best! He was relieved to return to find Leah had stepped up and done the requested chores. No need to berate her over her attitude, no need to nag her to get things done. The message he gave by removing himself to create a pause and staying calm and clear about what he expected communicated to Leah his confidence in her ability to be responsible for herself. These were small moments amid lots of challenges, and as we kept our attention on these small successes, Steve's confidence as a parent began to grow.

Elizabeth discovered she could directly influence a family day at the park by focusing first on herself. Their eldest, Erin, declared in a rude and unkind way that she was NOT going to join her family on their outing. In the past, Elizabeth would have argued, scolded, begged, and nagged in the hopes of having Erin join them, and ended up feeling sour about the interrupted family time. Now Elizabeth let pause step up for her. She did not interrupt Erin's tirade, and all the while let her self-talk encourage her to stay quiet. Elizabeth found herself saying, "Okay. You know where we'll be and we'd love to have you join us if you change your mind." And off the rest of the family went. Elizabeth used the walk to the park to vent to Steve—another pause that let her sort through her feelings. Once at the park, calmer and enjoying themselves, Steve and Elizabeth reached out to Erin one more time via phone—"Join us if you'd like, we are having fun!" And when Erin actually showed up, Elizabeth was stunned. No cajoling, nagging, or yelling required. Elizabeth and Steve welcomed her, Erin joined in, and everyone had a great time together. Elizabeth's commitment to pause took what could have been a relationship-depleting experience and a family time turned sour and turned it into a deposit into more healthy and positive relationships.

Self-care was at the forefront during our early sessions. By taking the time to focus on what could fill their accounts, Steve discovered how important quiet was to him. He'd intentionally look for moments that felt good to him—when he was out raking by himself, taking a walk, even hiding out in his bedroom. Elizabeth found times just with Steve to fill her account. They made a point of stopping off for coffee after taking the kids to school, of walking together to the store, of sitting in the car with their sleeping six-year-old in the backseat, just talking for a few minutes. As they took time to make deposits into their self-care accounts, they discovered they felt more connected, more of a team. They were more likely to pause by reaching out to each other before they responded in a heated situation. Steve found himself pulling the car over when his girls were in a LOUD dispute in the backseat, stepping out of the car and calling his wife. Elizabeth found she'd join Steve in the bedroom to purge her frustrations...and was far more able to then interact with her sassing teen or uncooperative six-year-old in a clear and calm way.

As a result of their work in Discovery, Steve and Elizabeth felt stronger. They found they could begin to see through the chaos to what was working—no matter how little the moment. As their self-care became a priority and their pause muscle strengthened, they discovered how much more of a team they became. And as their team building grew, they communicated solidarity to their children, which rippled out to more cooperative, connected experiences. Their girls could count on them to keep it together even as they could not—to be calm and available no matter the size and cause of the tantrum or other chaos. Focusing first on themselves was a powerful step to take, one that created a solid foundation for creating the calmer, more respectful and cooperative household they wanted.

It's Your Turn!

Discovery in your life

Now it's your turn. Think about what brings you to this book—what is it you'd like to be different about your parenting experience? Would you like more confidence? Kids who are respectful and cooperative? Do you want to feel calmer and more in control? Do you wish for relationships you relish? Now think of the times when you felt most confident, when your kids were respectful and cooperative, when you felt calm and in control. This is an energizing process, discovering what is working for you—where things are feeling especially good. We get to focus on times you've most enjoyed with your kids; times you felt really good about how you or your kids behaved in a challenging situation, times that stand out to you when your child was being just what it is you want more of—cooperative, a good listener, respectful, successful in school, a good friend, joyful and engaged with life and family, connected in a warm and wonderful way with you…

Steps for you:

Take each of these steps to help you discover what is working, where things (including you!) have been at their best, and what you can appreciate. Focusing on one or two at a time for several days to a week can have the biggest impact. Take your time—this is a process of change that needs the respect of time in order for you to truly create the kind of experience and relationships you want. Use the blank pages provided following each section to write your thoughts, ideas, and reflections—to do your work!

Parenting Inspired

1. **Notice what puts a smile on your face this week.** Maybe it is how a driver let you in on the highway, the spontaneous hug your son gave you, a glorious sunset, the sweet way your three-year-old's bottom lip quivers just before the tears flow ☺. Write these moments down; notice how it feels to think about and intentionally look for them.

2. **Do something, just for you, to deposit into your self-care account.** Little (what can you do, just for you, with only a minute to spare?) or big (those workouts at the gym, the date night with your spouse), they all count. Notice how it feels to intentionally focus on what feels good to you, how it supports you in being at your best. (See the Design section for a list of self-care ideas to inspire you!)

3. **Ask your parenting partner to create a list of what you do well, what your strengths are, what they appreciate about you**. If you are single, have a friend help or do it for yourself. Take your time with this; it can feel uncomfortable at first to write about yourself in this way, or to be writing for another. Think about things you take for granted—that your spouse always picks up the bath mat after their shower, dinner is usually together and at the table, you can be super organized with daily tasks, you can be counted on to read books at bedtime, lunches are made every day for your school-aged child, you never miss a school event. Think about what it takes to do these things—for instance: consistency, commitment, planning, flexibility, patience. These are strengths—and they can be your best friend as you move forward with creating the change you want! (See the Dream section for a larger list of strengths.)

4. **Intentionally notice all that your child does well and what you can appreciate about him or her.** Reframe what feels like negative qualities into positive ones—from "He's stubborn" to "He has real conviction" or "She sure can persevere!" Turn the "I'm going to do it MY way" into a sign of increased

independence, the mess left after a project as the evidence of great focus and passion. Appreciate the fact they got 60 percent of their spelling words correct and worked hard to do so, that the sticky kitchen floor was a result of your toddler diligently sponging up all the milk she spilled (and had fun squishing and swooshing the sponge in the milk puddle!) Notice how your child gets excited over reading, is generous with a friend, can share certain things well, builds the most intricate Lego structures (even if they take up the entire family room floor…) What you focus on grows, so looking to what your child does well and all you can appreciate about him or her is essential for encouraging more of these qualities—and it can leave you feeling far more optimistic!

5. **Pay attention to when you feel best about how things unfold with your child**—whether it is a heated moment that works out well or time together that is delightful. Take a moment and think about what strengths of yours stepped up in these instances (patience, resilience, creativity…) and how you were feeling. Throughout the week, write down what worked well, and record your strengths at these times and how you felt. Calm? Connected? Confident? Relieved? Excited? Lighter? Hopeful? Clear? Proud? Be as specific as you can.

6. **Reflect on the times when you have felt the most confident, joyful, calm, or at ease as a parent**. Let your thoughts rest on reliving these times. Think about what the particular time looked like, what was happening, what you and your child were doing and saying to each other. Consider your list of strengths and identify the ones that benefited you the most during these successful times. Or maybe discover new strengths to add to your list! Most importantly, reflect on what other feelings/qualities highlighted these times. **Write them down.**

Now, take a moment and consider this—if the feelings/qualities of these moments when you felt confident, joyful, or calm and at ease were in place in your current challenge, what could be different? What might you be doing or saying? How might it influence your child?

7. **Take time to notice when your specific strengths step up over the course of the week.** You know you can be patient as you wait for your preschooler to tie his own shoes. Where else does your ability to be patient step up? You know you can be counted on to have dinner for the family most nights or read books to your kids daily—in what other areas can you be counted on? You feel confident in creating a working bedtime routine—where else does confidence lead the way? Where else do you have a routine in place that works? *What you focus on grows,* so let's keep what works well for you up front and center!

8. **Practice pausing!** Notice what works for you to create a pause—perhaps breathing, encouraging self-talk, or walking away—go back and reread the list earlier in this section. Notice how your pausing influences situations, how you feel, and what is different for you as a result.

A bit of encouragement for you...

Maybe you are feeling overwhelmed or anxious as you read through this. Change—or the potential for change—can be unsettling. Know that your self-awareness is a strength! Let it remind you to pause...and perhaps focus solely on doing something just for you or on the things that put a smile on your face. Rest in this for a number of days and then come back. I think you will find you feel calmer and ready to move forward once again.

I encourage you to take the time to "try on" the steps that resonate the most with you and see how they feel. Give it several days—in a coaching relationship a parent often takes a week to focus on one or two steps at a time. Success can be achieved far more effectively with small steps—little bits at a time—rather than big ones. After you've focused on one step at length, revisit your anxiety, concerns, or frustrations and notice what is different—I will venture to say you will feel calmer, a bit more at ease, empowered to continue discovering. And remember, have fun! This really is a time for you—a time to grow yourself so you can be your best as a parent.

A page for your Discovery work....

Time for Reflection...

Now that you have taken time to focus on some or all of these Discovery steps, it is equally important to pause and reflect on the following questions. Use the space provided for your reflections:

- **What thoughts or feelings came up for you as you put different steps into practice?**

- **What did you notice was different as you focused on each step? How did it influence you, your child, or a situation?**

- **Which step(s) had the greatest impact on you? What might you like to do more of?**

- **What qualities of yours stood out the most in the steps you focused on and felt good about?**

The Power of Discovery

I think you may discover that—as you focus on what puts a smile on your face, on caring for YOU, on where you or your child does well, on all that is working—you will find yourself relaxing, breathing more easily, feeling a bit better. You may notice things improve—perhaps in small ways such as feeling a bit stronger and more patient through at least part of a tantrum, or in bigger ways such as a calmer week overall.

A bit of my story to share before you move on...

In my own Discovery phase, I found when I focused solely on pausing before answering my stubborn and reactive (I suppose she learned that from me...) teen daughter, I felt calmer and was more able to listen. As a result, she felt heard and respected. Our usual heated exchanges shifted. She surprised me when she started to work with me on compromises—something that had rarely happened before. She'd come back later, following my pause and initial calm response, and actually say, "I get it, Mom, I get what you said. Can we...." It blew me away. I know it should have been obvious to me long before how to create more of these win/win conversations—but as you know, when your button gets pushed, all bets are off. I am eternally grateful for *The Power of Pause* entering my life—and I can say with certainty that pause has influenced everyone I've worked with in simply amazing ways.

As we focus on what warms our hearts, where we are at our best, what we can appreciate about even the toughest moments, we begin to calm down, experience a bit more joy, and feel a bit more confident. This ripples out in meaningful and often huge ways over time. As you reflect on the steps you've taken—on the ones that resonate the most—notice what shifts for you. *What you focus on grows.*

Dream

Let's Dream!

Now it's time to gather the affirming "ingredients" of your successes—the qualities, feelings, and strengths that were in place when things went better or well with your children. Those times you noticed you felt the most confident, when your kids did listen well and behave better, when you felt the most calm and in control; times with your kids that felt simply fabulous. Let's gather them up and imagine how life can be different with these qualities, feelings, and strengths in place right now—rather like mixing up a new recipe with preferred ingredients ☺. This is the time for "thoughtful wishing,"[1] for creating your "end in mind"[2] or preferred future. With your Dream in place, you can be clear on where you intend to head on your parenting journey, making it more likely you can take action today that supports the growth of your Dream. Some like to call it their flight plan, a guiding North Star, or their "end in mind"—whichever way, no matter how tough times get and how off course you can feel, you will have your destination in mind. Now you can more easily set yourself back on track, headed toward your Dream…growing your confidence and joy along the way!

Using visualizations in this section of the book, you can create a Dream statement that truly resonates with you—one that is based on the affirming "ingredients" of your successes, and fills you with hope and a "YES" feeling from deep down within. What a way to empower yourself to create just what you want more of!

Story Time!

Listen to how our parents grew their Dream

Tom and Sarah

Tom and Sarah discovered that the times Erik was most successful with managing school-work and being responsible, the times they felt especially good about the choices he made, when they took pride in staying calm and even-keeled, were highlighted by *light-hearted humor, clarity on what was expected, confidence in themselves, teamwork as parents, and calm connection with their son.* They spent time on a visualization in which they imagined Erik in his twenties, ultimately describing the kind of relationship they hoped to have with this young man. This led them to their Dream statement:

"Our family enjoys light-hearted, warm, respectful times together. We stay calm and considerate as we listen well and work together as a team. Our son is responsible, competent, and productive as he moves through his school year."

This captured for them just what they wanted the most in their relationships and for their son. Reading it energized them, gave them hope and encouragement, and had them reflecting on the successes they had already achieved. Keeping their focus on their Dream led them to create and take steps (the

Design phase of this journey) that felt right and good to them, actively supporting and guiding them toward living their "end in mind."

Mary

Mary discovered that the times she felt best as a parent—times when she felt confident, in control, and delighted in who her kids were becoming—were highlighted by her staying *calm and connected with her children, being present to them, remaining clear on her expectations, and being aware of and communicating confidence in their abilities.* We spent time on a visualization of meeting up with the adult Jake and Olivia in a restaurant. She saw them as warm and caring, eager to share with her, confident in themselves. This led to Mary capturing the essence of this visual combined with the qualities of herself when she felt best as a parent. Her Dream:

**"I am a confident and calming influence on
my children as I encourage their growth as
cooperative, caring, fun, and capable individuals.
We are joyful and connected as a family."**

This stirred up such positive, deep feelings for Mary—it truly energized and empowered her daily. She now knew clearly what she wanted the most for her family, what kind of relationships and family life were important to her, what kind of parent she intended to be. This led to her actively taking steps (supported through the Design phase of our coaching journey) that had her feeling confident she was influencing the growth of just the kind of adults she hoped for, the kind of family life that was important to her. Mary felt inspired and certain she was building the healthy, joyful relationships with Jake and Olivia she wanted the most.

Steve and Elizabeth

Steve and Elizabeth discovered that the times when they felt the most in control of themselves, parented as a solid team, and felt good about how they handled the inevitable conflict and emotional ups and downs of young children and teens, were highlighted by *calm connection, care and respect for themselves and their girls, letting go, and appreciation.* Our visualization of their future adults had them describing a meal-time filled with good humor, contentment, sharing, and pride in who their children were becoming. Capturing the essence of this visual combined with the qualities that had them at their best brought us to their Dream statement of:

"We take care of ourselves and feel content and confident as parents. We parent calmly and respectfully, feeling joyfully connected with our children. We parent as a team—encouraging, accepting, and welcoming the independence of our children. We have fun together!"

Steve and Elizabeth both felt the weight lift off their shoulders as this Dream resonated deeply with them. It created an image of a warm family gathering with young adults confidently going forward in their lives. Relationships felt solid. They knew their Dream could become more of their reality, for each of their successes reminded them of just this. They were ready to grow more of what they truly wanted—they felt empowered to pursue the difficult change and growth in themselves necessary to encourage the respectful, joyful, deeply connected relationships they desired.

It's Your Turn!

A Dream for you

Now it's your turn! Gather up the list you've created of the qualities, feelings, and strengths you've discovered as you've paid attention to all that IS working well for you and your children. Focus on the ones that stand out the most to you—the ones that have consistently been a part of all your successes, of what is working well. A list of three to five will set you up well for the next step.

Ideas to help you along:

Confident, calm, a good problem solver, relaxed, patient, persevering, stamina, humor, lighthearted, pause, self-care, intentional, a good planner, creative, proactive, letting go, going with the flow, resourceful, consistent follow-through, connection, clarity, organized, caring, compassionate, a good listener, can be counted on, respectful, matter-of-fact, at ease, fully present, content, flexible, engaged...

Now you are ready to choose the visualization that feels best to you and that will help you clarify just what you want the most, your Dream. Here are three that I use regularly in my coaching practice:

- **The Miracle Day** [3] helps you imagine your day with the qualities that stand out the most to you in place right now—those top three to five qualities that are a part of all your successes.
- **Imagine Your Child as an Adult** [4] is a short visualization of imagining time in a restaurant with your adult child.
- **Begin with the End in Mind** [5] is a lengthier, more detailed visual imagining your child as an adult.

You might find it initially uncomfortable to define how your adult child's life looks—this is okay. Know that this is less about the exact reality of their adult life (something that ultimately will be up to them) and much more about the qualities and characteristics you discover about your future adult as you describe what you think their life might look like. And it is these qualities that you can nurture in your child right now. For instance, as you open yourself to deciding just what kind of job your future adult might have—be it an electrical engineer, a musician, an elementary school teacher—you might realize that it is creativity, compassion, problem solving, or other qualities that stand out to you, that are important to you—and this is the clarity that can lead you to a Dream that truly is empowering.

Enjoy this time imagining! One father delighted in describing the backyard of his son's first home—full of broken-down motorcycles that his son enjoyed tinkering with. Another decided their future adult would be a ski bum and world traveler, working odd jobs to finance his passions; and another parent described a young woman who might become a marine biologist working with whales in Sea World. As you will realize, it isn't the actual education, job, or lifestyle that is important here, but rather the qualities and characteristics in your adult child that emerge as a result of your imagining. Thoughtful wishing that can lead you to just the kind of adult you hope to grow. Have fun with this process—it is your opportunity to dream with abundance! It can leave you smiling, laughing, and crying…all in a beautiful way.

**"Begin with the end in mind,
but let go of the final results."**[6]
~Hal Runkel

It is important to understand that our children
ultimately will decide for themselves what they will
pursue in life—for this is what we want, responsible
adults able to take charge of their lives. This means
letting go of what we envision while also letting
it be the power and influence for us to
parent well right now.

So go curl up somewhere comfortable, maybe take along a snack
or hot drink, choose the visualization that resonates with you the most,
and immerse yourself in thoughtful wishing. I think you may find it will
delight you!

The Miracle Day

Imagine a miracle occurred while you were asleep one night and everything is as you'd like it to be. You are (list your top qualities from your successes—such as calm, confident, proactive...); your relationships feel just as you'd like them to (again, list your top feelings from your successes, such as connected, joyful, content, respectful...); *all is in place.* You are truly waking up to all these qualities and successes as your norm. When you wake up:

1. How would you know this miracle occurred?

Consider and perhaps write down:

- What would be happening? Think about the morning, the day, your evening, and how it unfolds. Consider what your interactions would look and feel like. What might you be saying to your children, your spouse? What would you and they be doing?

- How would you be feeling throughout this Miracle Day?

2. How would your children and parenting partner know this miracle had occurred?

Consider:

- What would be different for them? How might they now be feeling?

- What might they notice about you, about the day?

3. What might others looking at you living this Miracle Day notice?

4. How might the evening now look—whether it was a work and school day or a weekend, consider how the day would wrap up with this miracle in place…and how you would feel as you slipped into bed that night.

Time to pause...

Before you move on to the reflection questions,
flesh out your Miracle Day fully. Really "see" how
things might be with everything you desire in place—all
that has been working for you; your successes and the
qualities and feelings that highlight them.

Think through an entire day and sit in this
experience to really soak it up. Take your time.
You, and this process of change you are in,
deserve the respect of time.

Imagine Your Child as an Adult

Imagine you are walking along a busy street in a well-kept town or city. It is a bright spring day and you breathe in the fragrance of the blossoms from the trees you pass. You soak up the warmth of the sun with a sense of exhilaration. The birds are singing and the people passing you are smiling and friendly. Everyone feels the gift of a beautiful day, you think to yourself happily. A glance at your watch tells you that it is fifteen minutes to noon. You have several more blocks to walk and you feel confident you will reach your destination in time.

As you walk, you are suddenly filled with intense pleasure, satisfaction, and almost overwhelming gratitude. Tears of joy begin to form at the edges of your eyes. You are going to meet with (put in name of your child/ren) who are now adults, and you are feeling so proud, happy, and blessed for the extraordinary young men/women they have become. You walk with a spring in your step, just anticipating the upcoming lunch you will have and the conversation you will share with these precious people.

As you continue, you think of the past and some of the challenges you overcame, of some of the difficulties your children overcame. Sometimes it was very, very difficult. Sometimes you felt like you would never, ever feel rested again; or like you would never, ever have time for yourself again. You smile as you think back on the parent you were, the one who did not always know all the answers, but always had a full heart and a determination to do the best for your children. You feel deep compassion for yourself back then. You see how hard you worked; how much you sacrificed. You feel deep empathy for yourself as this parent who gave so continually.

And now, now on this beautiful spring day, you feel the immense satisfaction of a job well done. Only good memories grace your mind as you see the restaurant up in the middle of the next block. Images flash through your mind of your babies; you feel them snuggle into you, and you feel the pure joy of looking at their little toes and fingers, and watching them sleep so contentedly. Then you see your children in elementary school at a school event and how you watched them and felt amazed that these delightful, lively kids were yours. Then you see yourself arguing; words you should not have said; words you could not imagine coming from your child's mouth directed at you. The pain; the tears, the hugs that followed.

As you open the restaurant door you spot your child/ren—sitting at a table, looking up from their menus at just the same time you are looking in their direction. They smile—big smiles—and jump up together to grab you in a group hug. You embrace and the tears flow. As you sit down across the table from these young men/women and talk up a storm, you notice that now, as adults, they have certain enduring qualities. As you look at each of them, you list them in your mind's eye. You observe that they are happy, creative, and engaged. They share freely with you of their trials and tribulations and successes. They talk to you with trust and respect, to each other with lighthearted, joyful connection. Your heart swells even further. You delight in being with them.

A part of you now gets up and moves to a corner of the restaurant. You watch your older self and adult children talking, sharing, laughing, appreciating one another, having fun together. You watch them together for a time and as you watch, you feel so grateful. So very, very grateful. You leave them there. You know it's time to come back. You walk out of the restaurant with a heart overflowing with joy. You feel at ease, peaceful, and confident—knowing that the future has unfolded as you have envisioned it.

You come back to the present fortified, refreshed, and energized to live fully, joyfully, and intentionally in the present.

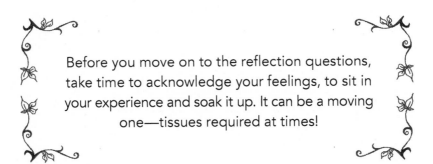

Before you move on to the reflection questions, take time to acknowledge your feelings, to sit in your experience and soak it up. It can be a moving one—tissues required at times!

Begin with the End in Mind...

Imagine your youngest at age twenty-five, and their siblings at whatever age that would make them...and ask yourself these questions. Answer each one as thoroughly as possible—embellish all you like; the richer your experience, the greater the impact. Keep your focus on all that you hope for, on what you want the most. This is meant to be your ideal—in your relationships, in your family life. Remember, this is "thoughtful wishing..."

1. Did they go to college? What were their majors? How about graduate school?

2. Are they married? Any children yet?

3. What kind of work do they do? Are they entrepreneurial, or part of a large corporation, or...?

4. What would their employers say about them? What kind of workers are they? What would their coworkers say about them?

5. How is their alone time spent?

6. What do they most like to do together with their friends?

7. What would their friends say about them? How would they describe them?

8. What do you see as some of their outstanding qualities or characteristics?

Now, imagine you were to get together with these adult children of yours, and answer these questions:

1. Would you be all together, or meeting with them individually?

2. Where would you be?

3. What would you be doing?

4. What do interactions look like? Think about what you'd be talking about and sounding like, and describe.

5. What else might be happening?

6. What are you thinking about as you spend time with them?

7. Finally, how would you be *feeling* during this get-together with your adult children? How might they be feeling?

Before you move on to the reflection questions, take time to acknowledge your feelings, to sit in your experience, to soak it up. It can be a moving one—bring out the tissues!

Time to Reflect...

...on your visualization, your thoughtful wishing, your Dream

If you chose **"The Miracle Day,"** here are a few more questions to mull over (use the following blank page for your thoughts and reflections):

- What might your family be doing differently if this miracle was the norm?

- How could living this Miracle Day as the norm benefit you a year from now—what might be different? Consider:

    o How your family life might look
    o How your professional or personal life might change
    o What your relationships look and feel like

- As you consider your Miracle Day, what word or words best describe the relationship you have with your children?

- What image comes to mind as you reflect on your Miracle Day? Is it playing together as a family, being outside, sitting together around a table for mealtime? The image evoked by your ideal day becomes a powerful influence for living your Dream—and can be what first comes to mind as you focus on just what you want more of, so take a moment and think about what picture comes to mind as you capture your Miracle Day in your mind's eye.

If you chose **"Imagine Your Child as an Adult" or "Begin with the End in Mind,"** then take time to think about these reflection questions:

- What image comes to mind as you think about your visualization, about your time together with your adult children? Seeing it clearly allows it to become a more powerful influence.

- As you consider your get-together, what word or words would best describe the relationship you have with your adult children?

- What are you doing right now to nurture the growth of the qualities you see in your adult children?

- What are you doing right now to grow young adults wanting and willing to spend time with you?

Dream

A page for your reflections...

Break time!

Remember, this journey you are on is a process. Put the book aside often and let your thoughts and experience "percolate" for a while. No hurry—real and lasting change takes time. Now, go do something just for you and when you are feeling ready to move forward, this book will be waiting for you!

Let's Build Your Dream!

Now we take the essence of your visualization, combine it with the strengths and qualities of your successes, and create a statement that brings you hope, energizes you, and evokes a clear image that resonates deeply, leaving you with a "YES" feeling from deep down within. Statements should be in the present tense and are most effective when kept to a few sentences. Easier to remember! Here are a few ways you can begin:

I am/We are…

My/Our family is/enjoys…

I live/We live…

I thrive/We thrive…

My/Our family feels/shares/thrives…

I/We parent…

I/We enjoy…

Let your sentences capture how you intend to feel, how the relationships look, and perhaps how you hope things can be for your children. Take your time and just start writing; paragraphs can later be edited and honed to truly capture what you want the most in just a few sentences. Be sure to play with your sentences as they emerge. Keep writing and rewriting (a page for your work follows shortly) until you have a few that resonate deeply with you, that call up the image of your visual, that leave you feeling "Yes!" from deep within you.

Ideas to get the juices flowing:

We parent with calm confidence as we encourage our children's growth as responsible, caring, productive individuals...

We parent with ease as our family shares positive, connected, joyful experiences...

We parent as a team, present and engaged with our children...

We are calm, connected, and caring as a family...

My family thrives as we support and encourage each other, growing as strong, capable, respectful individuals...

My family enjoys open and honest communication as we take the time to...

My children feel understood, encouraged, and empowered as I...

My child and I are content as we share a respectful, loving relationship...

My family thrives on many adventures together...

I live content as I calmly and confidently guide my children...

I thrive as I take care of myself...

I breathe with ease as I go peacefully through my day...

I feel energized, creative, and connected as I parent my children...

I live with purpose each day, centered and present to myself and my family...

I am lighthearted and thoughtful as I guide my children with calm confidence...

I am centered and confident as I parent with calm connection...

I guide with calm assurance, love, and faith as my children become strong, productive, and caring individuals...

Using your top qualities and feelings from all your successes will give you a statement that represents a preferred future you **can** live—for it will be *built on all that already is working for you, all that you intend to grow more of.* You may realize you already experience moments that remind you of your Dream—and when we move into the Design phase of this journey those moments can become more of your daily reality. *What you focus on grows.*

A page to work out your Dream...

An essential step to take...

Now that you have a Dream statement, write it up and post it where you can read it every day. I used sticky notes on the bathroom mirror, the microwave, and my desk. A client emailed it to herself every day so when she opened her inbox it was there, right in front of her. Another parent chose to have it in the car—just where he needed it the most.

Write it, post it, read it often. Tweak as necessary until it resonates deeply. Clarify the image it brings to mind—see it in your mind's eye in detail. Some parents enjoy creating a collage that represents their Dream—something beautiful to look at each day. Discover what works for you to keep your Dream at the forefront.

Now pause in your journey. Pause and take the time to focus on your Dream. Give yourself a few days...a week. Let it percolate until you feel ready to keep going. This is a process that requires time! *Notice what is different for you as a result.*

The magic of the Dream is in its power and influence.[7] When it truly resonates, feels right from all the way within, it has the power to drive you forward through even the toughest of times. The clarity it can provide has you more confidently responding in the now. My Dream—**"I am confident as I listen with care and guide my daughters with calm respect; we share deeply connected, joyful family times together"**—redirected my relationships with my teens in truly positive ways and brought a clear image to my mind's eye.

Alice's Dream Image

My adult daughters, husband, and I are gathered
around our little table on our boat out in our favorite
waters— Prince William Sound, Alaska. We are playing
cards— Hearts!—eating yummy food, laughing, joking,
competing in a somewhat serious but light-hearted
manner, sharing stories, feeling wonderfully
and joyfully connected.

As I navigated the tough moments and teen girl drama (of which
there was plenty!), the image of my Dream slowly began to lead the
way. I grew stronger in pausing, seeing us around that table, and feeling the deep joy and contentment my image triggered in me. It kept
me clear on the kinds of relationships and family life I intended to grow
and allowed me the opportunity to (more likely!) respond in such a
way that these future young women *would* want to spend time with
my husband and me—to play games, eat, and laugh together. I found
my Dream helped me calm down, listen with care, and respond more
respectfully. Even if my answer was still NO, my girls felt heard and
respected, for I had listened. I got better at accepting and letting go
of when I *did* get reactive, and using those times to think through a
do-over with my Dream in place, my calm and connected self in high
gear. Always it was my Dream that encouraged me, and even though
it was far from perfect at times, it kept me going and growing, getting
stronger and better in my relationships with my girls.

I will bet that you already put this ability to have a clear "end in
mind" into practice in ways you may be unaware of. I remember, long
before I knew of this process, heading out on errands with my baby
and preschooler and knowing clearly I wanted to be home before naptime so they could sleep in their beds (which also meant I'd get a

break, too!) With this clear "end" in sight, I made decisions based on it—I did only those errands that allowed us to return home in time, I had more patience as we worked our way through a store doing "one finger touches" and "eyes only" practice. I knew I wanted to return home with children who were more cooperative—and I could almost guarantee just that if I patiently let them participate on our errands. This was the power of having a clear "end in mind." And yes, more often than not I found success—we got home, had an easier transition with cooperative kids, and a naptime (for all of us!) that was satisfying. Being clear on what you want is a good thing—even if it is just napping in your own bed ☺.

Let your Dream statement and the image it evokes lead you. Let it influence every interaction, every decision you make. Let it step up to help you pause in challenging moments. Know that what we focus on grows—so keep your attentionon what you want the most.

As you focus on your Dream and the image it creates in your mind's eye, I think you will discover a strengthening of your relationships and experiences. They will begin to feel especially right and good. Just as I experienced with successful naptimes, more cooperative children, and teens who felt heard and respected, you, too, can enjoy the gifts of greater ease, joy, and confidence.

Now go write up your Dream, post it, read it often. Make a collage if you like. *Take your time in this—pause and relish just what it is you intend to grow.* From here we will design your way forward so that your "end" can become your now.

Design

Let's Design!

Here's where we get to roll up our sleeves and really get to work. You know where you want to go (your Dream!), you have a clear idea of your strengths and abilities that will get you there, and you already know what works for you and for your child. And I will venture to guess, if you've taken the steps in Discovery and Dream, you are already experiencing positive changes in your parenting and your relationships that feel good and right to you. Let's keep it going! Now is the time to take intentional action steps that work for you in order to grow your Dream. Enjoy reading what each of our parents we are following chose to do to further their Dream—what action steps they took that worked for them. Be encouraged and inspired as you do the same!

Story Time!

The designs of our parents

Tom and Sarah

With the clarity of their Dream, and the knowledge that they wanted to continue growing being calm and connected, to experience lighthearted family times, and to see their son move through his school year responsibly and productively, they embraced a number of steps that really were just extensions of all they'd already been doing:

- **Pausing** before making decisions, offering responses, interacting…and finding calm to lead the way. Like a muscle, pausing gets stronger with use.
- **Clarifying their expectations**—Having a clear framework within which Erik could make choices and respecting the choice he made was key for providing Erik with just the opportunities necessary to manage himself well.
- **Consistently following through** with the results of Erik's choices—Whether it was finishing his schoolwork on time and off to soccer they then could go, or deciding to skip his chores and discover he now couldn't afford to pay for the data on his phone. Sticking to the consequence they had clarified built Erik's trust that what Mom and Dad said, they meant.

- **Intentionally focusing on positive behavior**—By paying attention to where Erik was behaving in ways they wanted to see more of, to where strengths of his stepped up, Tom and Sarah found they could more readily calm themselves and see the positive changes occurring. This was encouraging! Authentically affirming Erik at these times was equally important—they found themselves saying, "Thank you for taking care of your cell phone payment. We appreciate that." Or, "It really helps when you get your own laundry put away!" *What we focus on grows.*

- **Teamwork**—Turning to each other for support and encouragement, giving each other time to pause as needed, and clarifying with each other what they wanted in each situation had Tom and Sarah feeling stronger in their partnership. A united front!

- **Self-care**—Regular, intentional "deposits" into their self-care account had them feeling more patient and resilient as Erik struggled, expressed feelings strongly, and otherwise navigated the bumpy road the teen years can be.

- **Posting their Dream and reading it every day**—This kept their "end" clearly in mind and helped them create the pauses, the reframes, and the ability to look for what they wanted more of instead of dwelling on the yuck. Empowering for both of them!

Tom and Sarah recognized the times they felt best about how they related with their son and the times he responded positively and respectfully was *when they stayed calm*. Exercising their pause muscle became the daily norm for them. With teamwork in place they were able to encourage each other along. When they felt their temperature rise, they intentionally took a break, or called each other, or brought their Dream image to mind. This led to calm connection with their son, which led to his listening and responding with more care and respect, stepping up on his own to help, and being proactive with his schoolwork. The times he tested were met with a matter-of-fact response and a commitment to following through with whatever expectation or consequence was in place. Erik increasingly knew he could count on his parents to keep it together even when he struggled, as well as to keep their promise[1] of following through with consequences for his choices. The trust this grew was tangible and the results spoke for themselves.

As Mom and Dad stepped back, let go, and became clear on what they expected—including growing the responsible young man they hoped for—Erik was given opportunities to manage his work and his everyday life without the constant nagging or yelling that once accompanied it all. Tom and Sarah began to lead with calm connection rather than anxiety-driven "We've got to get him to do it a certain way" disconnection.

Yes, Erik still forgot schoolwork, chose to drag his toes and wait too long to tackle his responsibilities, and made decisions that baffled everyone. But now Mom and Dad stayed calm, let him get upset, and found themselves asking him questions instead of dictating what they thought he ought to do. And now Erik began to take more responsibility for himself. The cool thing? How they felt as a family. Instead of evenings laced with anger and frustration, they laughed and talked. Instead of seething over choices made, they noticed what was going well. Erik felt less pressure and wanted to spend more time with them. Family time became just as they had dreamed—light-hearted, warm, and respectful. The bonus was how good Mom and Dad began to feel about themselves—they were increasingly confident and clear and found daily life to have more joy woven throughout. Their relationship with Erik began to thrive.

Mary

With the clarity of her Dream of being confident and calm, of growing cooperative, capable, caring children, and having joyful times as a family, Mary embraced a number of steps that supported her the most in living her Dream:

- **Pausing**—Whether she found herself hiding under the covers for a few extra minutes in the morning when Jake whined his way into her room, or literally biting her tongue and first observing her kids prior to responding—Mary focused on strengthening her pause muscle in creative ways.
- **Self-care**—Mary intentionally sought out opportunities to focus on herself in order to refuel—such as exercising more often and purposefully taking time to work on a quilt, sometimes with Jake and Olivia alongside sorting through fabric.
- **Creating fun opportunities**—The desire to find unique ways to encourage play had Mary acquiring a large, empty box and adding a few flashlights and books, singing along with her kids in the car rather than plugging them into an electronic device, and offering up games to play as a family. With her focus on "fun and joyful family times," Mary found she even enjoyed playing games that she was less enamored with because of the fun they created with her kids!
- **Asking questions, giving choices**—Instead of telling Jake and Olivia what she wanted them to do, Mary found that by asking them questions and giving them choices her kids cooperated more often: "It is time to leave in fifteen minutes. What does your backpack need in it to be ready to go?" "It's snack time—would you like to make your own snack or do you want my help?"

- **Noticing and affirming feelings**—Mary intentionally focused on naming her children's feelings in challenging moments: "You are frustrated…it makes you mad…I can see how sad you are…" Her kids felt heard and understood, empowering them to work through the challenge in more positive ways.
- **Clarifying expectations**—Being clear about what her kids could expect helped Mary to stick with the choices she gave them and follow through consistently with the consequences—or results—of their choices. Now Olivia and Jake could trust that what Mom said, she meant, leaving them feeling more secure and ultimately testing less.
- **Keeping her "end in mind"**—By posting and reading her Dream statement often, Mary found she stayed focused on what she really wanted, supporting her ability to pause, be calm, and find joy each day.
- **Creating opportunities for her children to be in charge of themselves**—Mary began to step back and let Olivia and Jake take more responsibility—making a snack on their own, choosing to wear four pairs of underpants(!), deciding for themselves if they wanted snow-boots or tennis shoes as they headed out to play. This left her children feeling more capable and confident—able to increasingly take charge of themselves.

Mary noticed, as she made deposits into her self-care account regularly, she felt calmer. With calm in place she found she could think more clearly and choose to behave in ways that supported her Dream. This led her to intentionally pause in a conflict, affirm Jake and Olivia's feelings, be clear on what their choices were, and consistently follow through. She found herself feeling more even-keeled despite rough transitions out the door with cranky kids; she discovered creative ways to respond to potential challenges that had her children behaving more positively—"I know you aren't ready to leave. You'd like to keep on playing! I know a fun game we can play once you are buckled in your seat..." "When your teeth are brushed and your jammies are on, see if you can come find where your stuffed kitty is waiting for you..."

Mary discovered real success in relaxing a bit and giving her kids a chance to be more in charge of daily tasks—sometimes requiring her to let go of having these tasks unfold exactly as she'd like ☺. She found when she gave Jake the opportunity to make his own snacks, he not only was creative in his combinations (those peanut butter and mustard sandwiches, carrots dipped in salsa, crackers folded up inside a slice of deli meat...), but he also ate his full share. The surprising bonus to this more engaged time together with her son leading the way at the kitchen counter? Upon finishing his snack he'd disappear to play on his own. In the past as she'd rush through throwing a snack on the table in order to get her kids outdoors to play, her kids would resist, complain, and whine—before, during, and after snack. Now? Off they went to play independently. Just what Mary wanted to encourage!

Morning transitions improved as Mary let go of taking responsibility for making sure Jake had his schoolwork or outdoor gear in his backpack. With the dream of growing competent, capable individuals front and center in her brain, she started asking Jake questions such as, "Do you have what you need packed for school?" and "Do you feel ready to roll? Okay, let's go!" This required Mary to let go of the fact that Jake sometimes forgot the work he was to take or the boots he needed to play at recess...and let Jake discover the results of this choice once he was at school. What ease this brought their mornings! No nagging, bribing, threatening—just questions and respect for her son's response. This led to Jake being more cooperative as he felt Mom's confidence in him. The best part for Mary was watching Jake take responsibility for his school papers—to, on his own, make sure they were stuffed in his bag, handed to his teacher, brought out at home to work on. Maybe not all the time (he was still quite young!), but as Mary stepped back and encouraged his independence, she noticed real growth emerge.

Mary's confidence grew as she found more and more success in calming herself, stepping back to let her children take increasing responsibility, and creating more joyful times as a family. She reveled in the cooperation within her family that emerged—including in her husband. I remember the time she shared when her family was on a road trip and, in the midst of the chaos erupting in the backseat, she turned to her husband and said, "We are joyful and connected as a family!" The twinkle in her eye spoke volumes to her husband; he, in turn, grinned back, and the chaos no longer defined their experience. What a benefit to the whole family!

Steve and Elizabeth

With clarity in place that they wanted to parent together calmly and respectfully, feel connected with their children, and be confident in encouraging Erin's, Leah's, and Kelly's growth as independent souls, Steve and Elizabeth took action. They focused on a number of steps that kept them encouraged and moving forward:

- **Pause**—Both Steve and Elizabeth found encouraging self-talk ("I can stay calm!"), focusing specifically on a chore, finding space to be quiet/take a break, and calling each other strengthened their ability to pause in the midst of conflict and challenge. The drive home from school pickup that had Steve pulling over, getting out of the car, and calling Elizabeth to talk himself through to a calmer place is an excellent example of the power pausing has. With the physical space he created and connection with his wife, he was able to calmly re-enter the car no matter the chaos of tired, hungry, arguing girls. Pause! It looks many different ways ☺.

- **Affirming feelings**—This became the mantra for both parents. When they first named their girls' feelings when dealing with an upset or conflict, they discovered that it not only created a pause for them, it kept the girls' upset feelings and behavior from spiraling up to the intense levels of the past—they felt understood.

- **Full presence**—Steve, especially, discovered positive change as he let go of distractions and focused fully on the daughter he was with. His girls felt heard and respected, and slowly the trust this built between them had his daughters turning to him as the resource he wanted to be. One-on-one dates were another way he gave Erin, Leah, and Kelly his full attention, depositing in positive ways into his relationship with each daughter.

- **Putting their attention on what they want more of**—Both parents began to let go of dwelling on negative behaviors and intentionally looked for what they wanted more of—responsible, independent, cooperative girls. They created more opportunities for their girls to be successful—sending Erin or Leah to the neighborhood store by themselves to pick up a few items, allowing their eldest to spend extra money with an agreement in place on how to pay it back, giving Erin and Leah chances to babysit Kelly for short amounts of time, letting Kelly take charge of making muffins (six-year-old style!) at the kitchen counter.
- **Clear expectations and calm, consistent follow-through**—With clarity on what they wanted the most, Steve and Elizabeth found they could give their daughters a clear framework with choices, and calmly and consistently follow through with the results of the choices their girls made. Nagging and threatening lessened; calm, respectful connection grew.
- **Teamwork**—Steve and Elizabeth found as they calmed down they were more likely to check in with each other first before dealing with a conflict with the girls. Now with a conversation and agreement in place regarding expectations and consequences, they became a united front with their daughters. No more playing Mom off Dad in their household!
- **Intentional family adventures/fun**—Park days, bike rides, family movie nights, one-on-one dates with each daughter, skiing adventures, picnics on the living room floor—these became a focus for the whole family and filled them in amazing ways.

- **Family meetings**—This became a key activity in family life. Whether it was a disagreement they needed to discuss or the fun plans for the day, they came together on the floor in the living room and shared ideas and concerns. Their girls felt safe, heard, and included; Steve and Elizabeth found this to be a tool that supported the respectful connection they wanted the most.

Steve and Elizabeth's confidence grew exponentially. They felt strong as a team and centered in their Dream. They found they could meet challenges with a calm presence, whether they knew the answer or not. Their eldest's first high-school dance came up in the midst of our coaching and though it created a lot of anxiety for both parents, they let their Dream guide them and focused on this as an opportunity for Erin to spread her wings a bit more. They worked together to come up with clear expectations for her, talked with her by asking questions and finding out her hopes and ideas, used the dress shopping as a chance for a one-on-one date with their daughter, and created an overall experience that had Erin glowing and both parents (relatively) comfortable as they dropped her off at the dance.

This repeated itself many times over—as a daughter presented a challenge, be it a reactive "You can't make me!," increased whining from their youngest, or a desire to do an activity that felt uncomfortable to Steve or Elizabeth, their growing ability to pause, calm themselves, communicate with each other, be clear, give choices...and calmly follow through with the results of the choice left them feeling confident they were headed in the right direction—toward their Dream. I appreciated how they came to realize they didn't need all the answers—just the clarity of how they wanted things to be and feel (their Dream). With this in place they could trust themselves to move forward in the right direction. Mistakes became do-overs; family meetings created the safe, respectful, connected place for everyone to share; and humor stepped up as they now could laugh a bit more about the trials and tribulations of parenting. They all felt empowered to create the family life they wanted the most!

It's Your Turn!

Design in your life

Now it is your turn. You get to let your Dream empower you as you choose steps to bring it closer to your current reality—you get to design your way to living your Dream! *What is your top priority to focus on that could bring you the greatest relief, satisfaction, or joy; that could best support you in living your Dream?* You may find it is different from what initially brought you to this book. It may be your desire to turn your toddler's or teen's button pushing into more cooperative behavior; maybe it's the continued practice at pausing so you can be calm, clear, and confident as you move through a challenging time with your child; it could be supporting your child through a tough school experience; perhaps it's the desire to get out of the house in the morning smoothly—with your kids successfully in tow and everything together(!). You have defined your overall Dream, and now it is time to focus on the steps that can make it happen.

Take a moment and consider:

- **If you were living your Dream 100 percent right now—what might your top priority look like?** What might be different about the button pushing, the morning transitions, your child's school experience? Consider what you might be saying or doing differently, what your child might be doing differently.

For me, my top priority was staying calm. I knew if I was living my Dream, then my desire to be calm would mean I'd be superb at pausing with my teens and always listening first—making it more likely they'd listen to me, as well. Now the button pushing would no longer be button pushing, for I'd be unfazed by it. I'd see clearly their growth as independent young women and find ways to support and encourage this. My calm and ease would bring them just what they needed—a positive, strong resource in me.

- **With your Dream in place and your top priority looking the way you'd like** (such as no more buttons being pushed, smooth exits from the house and feeling calm as the norm, totally confident and clear in all you do), **what thoughts and feelings are you experiencing at the end of your day?** I'd venture to say you fall into bed tired, content, and satisfied far more often. Perhaps with your attention on tomorrow rather than on rehashing all that drove you crazy today, you can actually go to bed feeling excited, prepared, and creatively thinking through how the next day will work. Or maybe just fall contentedly to sleep ☺. What a difference that could make.

Know that thinking through these considerations, much like you did in the Dream phase of the book, can energize you to take and stick with the steps you choose. Think often about how you'd like things to be, how they could be, and how you'd feel when they are going well, for *what you focus on grows.*

Now is the time to be very intentional about a step you wish to take as part of your Design—choose what resonates and focus on it for a number of days. *Again, this is a process and it deserves moving slowly and with care.* If you find you are feeling overwhelmed, it is a reminder to take a break. Time to take care of you!

Read through the following steps—they are ones that have consistently made a difference for parents—and consider your top priority for living your Dream. What step do you see yourself taking to make a difference? What strengths of yours will need to be in place to make it work? This stage is energizing and empowering for you are taking concrete steps toward your Dream. This also is the hard work, for it is asking you to create the change you want by sticking to these steps, no matter how your kids react. And they will react, for when we switch up what we usually do to something a bit different, it can shake up their world and be truly unsettling. When something is unsettling, kids tend to work even harder (a nice way of saying they'll act up even more!) at getting us back to the old (no matter how unproductive) patterns.

You are already well on your way to positive change due to your work through Discovery and clarifying your Dream. Now let's make it the lasting change you want the most!

Words of encouragement as you move forward...

Think of it like a dance...

As you actively create change, think of it as switching your dance step right in the middle of the dance. Our children—our dance partners—suddenly trip. Now they try, often with great flair and perseverance, to get us back to the old, familiar, albeit unproductive dance by testing and acting up more, ramping up the undesired behavior. Why? Because the old and familiar, no matter how bad it was, feels safe and secure to them.

...and keep dancing!

Stick to the steps you decide to take. Make a small
change of perhaps one "dance" step (much easier
to stick with when you keep it small!), and practice it
consistently for a number of days, a week, or longer
as needed. This gives your children the opportunity
to get familiar with it and to be able to count on the
new dance—which allows them to start feeling secure
once again. As they feel more secure they calm down,
and now real change (a new, productive dance!)
really can emerge.

Let your Dream statement empower you to
continue creating the positive change you want
the most—the "new dance" that has life flowing
in more joyful ways!

Design steps for the taking...

- **Self-care**—Make deposits often in little or big ways to keep your account full. Consider also what works best for you that feels good and only takes a few minutes. Being intentional about it is what makes it a deposit. Ideas from parents I've worked with include:

  o   Making a good cup of coffee or tea (drinking it can be a bonus!)
  o   Exercising at length—joining a gym, training for a race, walking your dog each day...
  o   Exercising briefly—doing a few yoga stretches, taking a quick, brisk walk around your garden or to the mailbox...
  o   Reading a short article
  o   Joining a mom's or dad's group—online or in person
  o   Calling a friend
  o   Going out on a date with your spouse/partner
  o   Standing in a hot shower for just an extra minute or so
  o   Sitting down with your feet up
  o   Spending a moment with a pet
  o   Moving forward on a project or craft—for a few minutes or longer!
  o   Enjoying a funny YouTube video
  o   Sitting quietly in the car before heading into home after work
  o   Getting outside—at length, to soak up sunshine, to breathe
  o   Working in the garden—even just to tend to one plant
  o   Turning off or covering your computer screen as you enjoy lunch at your desk
  o   Getting takeout for dinner

- **Pause**—Strengthen this muscle all day long! Practice it at work, on the road, in the grocery store, as well as with your children.

You know what works for you to pause—deep breaths, encouraging self-talk, focusing on a task, closing your eyes, etc. Focus on this intentionally and continue noticing how it supports living your Dream.

- **Teamwork**—Focus on being a team with your parenting partner:

    o Actively appreciate their ideas, their feelings.
    o Give each other the support to pause and do self-care—often!
    o Honor differences—as one parent said, "We may not be on the same page, but we are in the same book!"
    o Notice what feels like positive and productive teamwork.
    o Ask each other questions as you explore possibilities, challenges, and make plans. The respect this communicates carries directly over to your children.
    o Carve out intentional time together—go on a date, share a cup of coffee on the deck, take a walk together.

- **Create clear expectations and offer choices**—Be clear with your children on what they can expect about the day, a situation, family rules, etc., and give choices within these expectations. Examples include:

    o "We are leaving for school in ten minutes. You'll need your backpack, shoes, and jacket. What can you take care of?"
    o "Dinner in five! Can you please set the table or would you like to dish out the spaghetti?"
    o "In the store we use our eyes only or touch with one finger. If it is too hard, then you will need to ride in the cart."
    o "Home by eight, please, so you can keep having the privilege of using my car!"

o "When you talk like that I am unable to listen. Let me know when you are ready to use a respectful tone of voice."

o "Once the dolls are picked up you can join us for a game. If you choose not to help clean up, that's fine. Just know you will need to head upstairs to get ready for bed instead of joining our game."

o "I need help with cleaning. Which can you take care of—the bathroom or the entryway?"

o "Milk stays in the cup or is swallowed down to your tummy…"

o "Would you like one or two more turns before we head toward bed?"

o "Time to buckle up! Can you do it all by yourself, or would you like my help?"

A word about choices before we continue…

Giving and respecting our children's choices empowers them. Choice is how they learn what they are responsible for—that they are accountable for their actions. Choice is how they learn more about themselves—their likes and dislikes, what they can and cannot do, what is their responsibility and what is not. Choice can be inherent in situations—whether or not they listen, come home by curfew, follow the family rule of chores first, play second.

Choice can be intentional—when you ask if they want to wear the long- or short-sleeve shirt, if they want to buckle up by themselves or with help, if they feel like skipping across the parking lot holding hands or walking carefully beside you, if they want to do homework before or after dinner. How we respond to the choice they then make determines what is learned.

When we work hard at getting them to choose just
what WE want them to choose, things tend to get reactive—
we may nag, scream, bribe, or threaten. We may get compliance
in the moment from our children (and momentary relief!) but at the
cost of them really learning from their choice, for their attention
will be on our reactivity rather than on how they feel, what they like
or don't like, what is their responsibility. This undermines the inner
motivation necessary for managing themselves and
future choices well.

When we instead respect their choice by calmly and consistently
following through with the result of their choice (giving them the
time to buckle themselves if that is what they chose, taking away the
privilege of going out the next night because they chose to come
in past curfew), we are now empowering our children to learn from
the inside out—to figure out they really don't like missing out on
seeing their friends the next night because they broke curfew, to
find out that they CAN buckle all by themselves and now feel oh
so proud of themselves. This is real learning. This is respectful to
and empowering for a child. This builds healthy relationships,
more cooperation, and capable and competent kids.

- **Calm and consistent follow-through**—When we keep our promise by following through calmly with what we say we'll do, our children can count on us, and we build their trust in us. This includes following through with a promised treat or a lost privilege. It can sound like:

  o "You carried your plate all the way to the counter! Now you are ready to play our family game."
  o "I can see it is too hard to keep the milk in the cup or swallowed down to your tummy. Time to be all done." And the cup gets put away...

o "You buckled all by yourself! Now we can go."

o "You really don't want to be buckled at all. Time to buckle and be safe. I will do it for you."

o "All ready! Thank you for gathering your jacket and backpack. We are headed out on time!"

o "It seems it's too hard for you to get your backpack ready. It's time to go." And off you go, perhaps minus the backpack (and now your child has the opportunity to discover that minus his backpack he doesn't have his lunch or homework, hopefully influencing him the next morning to be more likely to gather all he needs…).

o "You chose the blue cup! Here you go."

o "You'd rather have the green cup, but it is dirty. When you are ready for your drink, let me know. The blue and red cups will be on the counter."

o "Thank you for coming home by eight. I appreciate you respecting the rules."

o "You chose to come home late. I can tell you had a great time, but know that my car will be off limits to you until Sunday."

o "You chose one more turn! Thank you for being ready to head upstairs. Now we may have time for an extra book tonight."

o "Two more turns just didn't feel like enough. I can tell you are disappointed. It is time to head upstairs. I can carry you or you can run up as fast as you can."

- **Daily affirmations**—Use your strength at "encouraging self-talk" to reframe thoughts to just what you really want. When you catch yourself saying, "This is going to be a rough day!" change it to, "Today is going to be full and busy, and I intend to move through it calmly and confidently." If you find yourself saying, "He's pushing my button and I'm going to lose it!" change it to, "He really is exploring just what he can and cannot do—I can stay calm as I help him through this." This can be a powerful step—it is putting your focus on just what you want, rather on what you don't want. Writing down your affirmations can help you strengthen this ability as well. What you focus on grows!

- **Full presence**—Put aside distractions to give your child your full attention, whether it is for a few minutes before you focus again on your chore, or at length. When we give our kids our undistracted presence, they feel heard and know they are important to us, and are more able to then respect when we need to give our full attention to something else. Here are some ideas:

    o Put screen/electronic devices away, silence them, or turn them off so they are less likely to distract you while you tend to, play with, or talk to your child or teen.

    o Be clear about how much time you need to finish something, finish, then intentionally join your child—just as you promised.

    o Turn fully to meet your child's eyes even if only to say, "I hear you want me to play. I need to finish my e-mails/ stirring the sauce. When I'm done, I will join you." Then turn back to your e-mails or sauce…this is instead of typing or stirring away as you say over your shoulder, "I'm coming, I'm coming!"

    o Pause and kneel down and touch your child as they tell you something.

    o Take a real camera on the family adventure so your smartphone can't lure you in to other activities besides taking photos ☺. Wear a watch for similar reasons….

    o Be prepared for your teen's odd hours of wanting you to be present—in the car, late at night, just as you are rushing out the door. Do what you can to pause and really listen, even briefly—your willingness to let go of your rush speaks volumes to your teen—and eventually makes it easier to let them know you can listen better after a good night's sleep, when you're back from your errands, when you are no longer in a rush.

o Offer one-on-one opportunities with each child—a date to do something they want to do. This fills our children's buckets immensely and can then create more time for you to focus on all the other things needing your attention—all because your child feels loved, connected to you, respected, and enjoyed. And maybe sound asleep out of pure exhaustion, thanks to your adventure together!

- **Notice and affirm positive and neutral behaviors**—What we focus on grows, so intentionally put your focus on what you want more of, on what your child does well. It may sound like:

  o "I see how hard you are working on your project. That is taking quite a bit of concentration!"
  o "You and your sister played the board game for a long time together. I bet you both had fun."
  o "I can see how grateful your brother is for your help with his homework. That was really thoughtful of you."
  o "Your plan to tackle your homework after soccer practice worked well for you. I bet it feels good to know it's done and you have time to hang with your buddies!"
  o "Thank you for handing me your plate. I appreciate your help in clearing the table."
  o "I appreciate you using your words to tell me about how mad you feel. Let's see what can help you get your mad out and feel better."
  o "The living room looks great! It really helps me to have it tidied up, thank you."
  o "I appreciate you calling to let me know you'll be late. That really was respectful of my time and I want you to know that."
  o "I know you can sleep soundly all night long, tucked cozily in your bed…"

- o "I know your sister really appreciated you sharing your dress with her. I can see how excited she is to wear it tonight!"
- o "What a kind thing to do for our neighbor! I know how much it means to him."
- o "Wow! You made it to the top of the climbing toy. I saw you keep trying and trying...and you did it."
- o "I appreciate you waiting until I was done talking with Daddy. That took patience!"

- **Plan and organize**—For many parents this can be key for feeling calmer and able to be present to their children. Let your proactive self step up and have a plan in place or things already organized for easy implementation. Now cooperation can more likely be the name of the game due to your feeling more in control, calmer, and able to be fully present. Here are a few ideas to keep you organized:

  - o Wake up fifteen minutes earlier to get some self-care time in or to have things in order prior to waking the kids.
  - o Have a bag of healthy snacks available in the car to fend off hunger after school or daycare.
  - o Simplify by packing away half the toys—rotate them through every few weeks and they become "new" all over again!
  - o Set up a few of your child's toys in a unique way after they go to bed at night—this can engage them in different kinds of play the next morning, giving you extra time. Try lining up their toy animals in a line across the living room floor ("Look! Your animals are having a parade!"), setting up a saucepan, spoon, and some dry beans for "cooking" on an upside-down box on the kitchen floor, or adding a few special books, sleeping bags, and flashlights to the blanket fort they've been

playing in. Have fun with this. We found great success with a cardboard tube taped to the wall at an angle and a basket of small rubber balls next to it...all kinds of independent play evolved from sending those balls racing down the tube!

o Prioritize your have-to lists and errands—this can lend itself to a calmer experience when you minimize what you really have to get done, rather than trying to cram it all in no matter the cost (often very cranky kids...).

o Tackle just one pile of office items at a time, rather than trying to organize the entire room all at once. Now you can feel accomplished and a little less chaotic...and this can influence your whole day (and relationships!) in a positive way.

o Use a chart for the family to follow what chores each is responsible for, what they can expect as they participate in daily jobs or activities, what the after-school/before-dinner responsibilities are. Charts of different kinds can work for some families—discover if it helps yours.

o Let teamwork step up as you talk through plans with your parenting partner—whether it is for a trip to the park or just how the day needs to unfold. By getting clear about the plans ahead of time, no mixed messages are given to your kids and cooperation often increases.

o Start having family meetings—gather together regularly or as needed and listen to everyone's ideas. This can lead to a well-planned and organized adventure or to a positive and productive response to a conflict.

- **Notice what puts a smile on your face**—Intentionally notice what makes you smile! Write these moments down, reread them on days that are more difficult. Include things that may have nothing to do with your children. As we put our attention on what feels good, we can feel good. And now we are in a position to interact more positively, communicate more respectfully, relax and let things roll off our shoulders a bit more easily. Something that can work well is keeping favorite baby photos around as your children grow. Looking at them can bring a smile to your heart just when you need it the most, influencing you in lovely ways.

- **Create a collage of your Dream**—Collect photos, drawings, and colors that depict your Dream and create a collage that you can look at often. For those of us who are truly visual folk, creating a collage is powerful. Just collecting photos has our attention on what we want more of, and makes the finished product satisfying and energizing. Have fun with this!

- **Create intentional opportunities for increased independence**—It is always a benefit to re-evaluate where you can increase chances for your child to be in charge of him or herself. So often acting up that pushes our buttons is due to a child working hard at being more independent. Look to areas where your child already takes charge of him or herself and consider how you can increase these opportunities. A few ideas to get you thinking:

  o **Cooking opportunities**—Children of all ages like to roll up their sleeves and work at the counter with you. Toddlers and preschoolers can knead bread dough, pour and mix ingredients, crack eggs, spoon muffin batter into muffin tins; elementary kids like to plan meals, help collect the ingredients, and then put it all together; teens love to have the kitchen to themselves and a few friends—baking, making dinners, trying out the new smoothie recipe.

  o **Getting dressed**—Little ones can have more chances to decide what they want to wear, whether you offer three shirts to choose from, or let them totally take charge as they dig through their drawers, wrangle on those socks, and decide on a ballerina dress to wear to swim lessons; older kids and teens can be given more responsibility with what they choose to buy and wear, as well as when they decide to actually do their laundry!

o **Care of their bodies**—Whether it is letting your toddler squish the washcloth and take care of scrubbing his own tummy, respectfully allowing your preschooler to use the bathroom "all by myself," giving your elementary child the chance to braid her own hair, or supporting your teen's newfound interest in a vegan diet—there is always room to increase opportunities for our children to be in charge of their bodies, ultimately empowering them to take responsibility for how they care for themselves.

o **Daily tasks**—Every single task done with your child, from getting ready in the morning to climbing into bed, can be a time to step back a bit and let them be more in charge. Look to what tasks you do automatically and consider what part of them your child can take charge of, always considering their age, stage, and abilities. Include them often, and offer choices and jobs you can feel good about—the kind where it is okay if it ends up less than perfect or a mess. They won't always make the choices we would and that is often okay—even necessary for real learning! Forks can be put into dishwashers in the wrong direction; jammies don't always have to be actual jammies; the dog's food dumped into the water bowl just makes for a soupy dinner for Fido (or something fun to strain out and try again!). Vacuuming can miss a few spots, school lunches made can have some interesting combinations. The key is, include your child—and be creative and willing to let go a bit as you do so. What a way to support the growth of a self-directed, responsible future adult.

- **Intentional Family Fun and Adventures**—Create more opportunities for what brings you joy with your children. This can include big adventures that require planning, lots of time, teamwork (an all-day hike or a trip into the city to explore the Aquarium…), or small ones such as having a picnic lunch on the floor, or a water fight as you wash the car, or heading to the park after dinner. Maybe it is a sing-along during a lengthy road trip, or an "I Spy" game at the dinner table. Board games, running-around games, wrestling-together games. Discover ways to create more fun— more joy—as a family! The memories are priceless…and often bring laughter and connection as they are reflected on over the years ☺. They are gifts that keep on giving…

Remember…

Discovery gave you the opportunity to see what works for you and what you want to do differently. Your Dream clarified what it is you really want the most. The steps you choose now, in Design, are based on what already works for you. Now you are more likely to stick to the step you choose and successfully create the change you want…actively growing your Dream. Always pause, reflect on what is working, be open to tweaking your step, and try again as needed!

This is a growth process, and it has its own timeline. As you take a small step that feels right to you, pay attention to what unfolds, what is different for you, and how it works to grow what you really want— your Dream.

A page to Design your way...

Time for Reflection...

- What step(s) made the most difference for you?

- What did you notice was different as a result of your step—how did it influence challenging situations, your children, and you?

- What strengths of yours benefited you the most with each step you took?

- What might you like to do more of, and how do you see it strengthening your Dream?

- What is your plan to care for yourself this coming week? (Remember, taking care of you is essential for parenting well...and with all this work, you deserve to make deposits into your self-care account in lovely ways!)

What you focus on grows...

What has reminded you of your Dream, even just a
little tiny bit? Look intentionally for those moments
that reflect just what you want the most.
Watch them add up!

Some thoughts before you continue...

In the Design phase of our journey to parent well and intentionally
we actively choose steps to realize our Dream, and we commit to trying things on for size. The cool thing is, after you've stayed with a step
consistently for days at a time, you get to decide if it works or not, and
then do it differently if you'd like. Think of knitting or sewing—how we
often pull out the stitches and rework our project until we like what we
have; or when we alter a clothing item to discover it still doesn't quite
fit...so off it goes and the next round of alterations is tried. We keep
at it, stay focused on what we truly want, and are willing to try and try
again until it looks, feels, and fits just right.

The Design phase is also a time for reflection and awareness—to
observe, be curious as you take a step, notice the impact, focus on
yourself and check in with how you feel, what is different for you. Take
your time...as you know, this is a growth process, one that works best
when given time. Just like with knitting or sewing, be willing to take
out the stitches and rework your parenting project! Slowly. Repeatedly.
With trust. Until it "fits" just right.

There are many steps you can take—the list here includes just the
ones that have come up most consistently throughout all the coaching
I've done. I want to emphasize the importance of taking small, doable
steps. If all you can do is affirm your child as he automatically buckles

his seatbelt after he climbs into the car, do it. Every day. Small steps can be the most impactful because they can create real change over time. Choosing a simple, daily affirmation can have your child feeling an inner sense of "I CAN!" that bubbles out and has them willing to take increased responsibility, feeling more cooperative, expressing their ideas openly and with glee. This can make your relationship feel so much better.

One couple discovered a surprising ease to the start of their days as they chose the small, simple step to call out from their bedroom to their preschooler when she woke—oh-so-cranky, each morning. They'd call out "good morning!" and let her know she was welcome to join them for a snuggle...and then they'd wait instead of hurrying to go to her with the intent of "fixing" her crankiness. This honored her ability to take charge of herself, put the focus on what they wanted more of (those wonderful morning snuggles!), and the really cool thing is that after practicing this new "dance step" together a few times, the cranky morning wake-ups transformed into cheerful family snuggles, starting their day off positively and with much more cooperation and joy. A small shift, and it rippled out in magnificent ways.

Keep your Dream at the forefront always. It is the clarity of where you intend to head that will encourage you the most as you take Design steps. Let it guide and empower you.

Destiny

Let's live your Dream!

What is reminding you of your Dream? Take a moment and think about the changes you've created and are creating, about how your relationships and family life now feel, what is truly different from when you began the journey this book has taken you on. Destiny is when you find yourself living your Dream more and more. Now you get to celebrate all the little and big changes you've created, all the things that feel right and good, all that is reminding you of your Dream. This is a time to intentionally acknowledge your growth—to toast yourself! You've worked hard, and the rewards are showing. Honor this—relish the increased confidence, joy, and ease you may be feeling. Breathe a sigh of relief over a calmer household. Know without a doubt that it is due to your commitment to growth. Let Destiny be a time you intentionally focus on all the positive changes you've created, *for what we focus on grows.*

Story Time!

Our parents' Destiny

Tom and Sarah

Tom and Sarah thrived! The confidence they grew in themselves and in their son changed the negative dynamics that brought them to coaching. Now when anxiety tried to take over (anxiety is something that never really goes away—it is truly a natural part of being a parent), they found relief with pausing, were empowered by their Dream, and as a result could manage their anxiety so it no longer led the way in their interactions with their son. With anxiety out of the way there was no need to battle, to nag, or to yell. There was little need to punish or direct. They were clear on the responsible, respectful, productive qualities they intended to nurture in their son, and with this clarity their anxiety over his teen antics calmed and they were able to respond to Erik in relationship-building ways. And Erik felt supported and encouraged—setting him up well for successfully moving through the high school years. Their family felt more deeply connected, and joy in their lives was tangible on a daily basis.

They shared what they felt was paramount for them to stay true to this course they were on—*to sustain and grow their Dream:*

- **Pausing** was at the top of the list!
- **Self-reflection**—Focusing first on themselves to think, reflect, and clarify what they wanted and how they'd like to feel.

- **Self-care** to keep a full account of resilience, patience, calm...
- **Letting go**—Instead of trying to control their son, they wanted to continue stepping back and giving him increasing opportunities to take charge of himself—to ultimately not sweat the small stuff ☺.
- **Teamwork**—Bolstered by intentional date time, they felt united with and supported by each other. Knowing they could really lean on each other to ease anxiety brought relief!

Tom and Sarah found they were living their Dream of **"Our family enjoys light-hearted, warm, respectful times together. We stay calm and considerate as we listen well and work together as a team. Our son is responsible, competent, and productive as he moves through his school year."**

Their commitment and perseverance through their own growth process had gifted them with the kind of relationship they wanted with their son—one based on calm connection, joyful family times, and a son who could count on his parents. Hearing from them a year after we finished working together that all was going well for them was evidence of their continued commitment to grow and parent well. A joy to hear!

Mary

Mary's confidence and joy in parenting grew tremendously. With confidence in place, she found that many of the things that drove her crazy when she first came to coaching were no longer such a big deal. Life calmed down for her, her sense of humor stepped up, and a lighter approach to all things children emerged. Mary shared what she felt was key for her to stay true to this course she was on—*to sustain and grow her Dream:*

- **Pausing**—Truly a lifesaver for Mary! It always helped her recenter and calm herself.
- **Reading her Dream statement often**—It continually encouraged and empowered her.
- **Self-care**—Regular exercise and intentional space apart from her children was key for Mary to parent well—to be calm, confident, and connected with her children.
- **Noticing and affirming behavior she wanted more of**—Mary knew intentionally keeping an eye on when her children were caring, capable, cooperative, etc., reinforced the behavior she wanted the most.

More and more often Mary found herself living her Dream of **"I am a confident and calming influence on my children as I encourage their growth as cooperative, caring, fun, and capable individuals. We are joyful and connected as a family."**

Her ability to persevere, to find the humor in situations, to always refocus and try again led her to enjoy the antics of her children and see how caring and capable they were becoming. She felt calmer, steadier, and happier. Friends and family noticed how things were going more smoothly, regular babysitters were planned so Mary could keep her self-care more easily in place, and family time was created by playing card and board games together. Mary felt in control and calm; her joy in and appreciation for the ups and downs of parenting rippled out to her family, encouraging the joyful and connected experiences she wanted the most.

I had the privilege of coaching Mary several times over a number of years. Tune-ups, as I like to call subsequent coaching sessions, reinforce just what a parent is striving for and give them more consistent practice at the tools they've acquired. They are a time to strengthen the muscles that help them the most. As a result of this increased focus and practice, parents can often regain the balance in their family life more quickly. With her coaching tune-ups, Mary rediscovered her calm, balance, and sense of humor more quickly, and the joy and connection with her children would soon follow. She now lights up as she shares with me both the joy and the troubles her parenting journey brings. Her confidence in herself is a joy to see!

Steve and Elizabeth

Steve and Elizabeth's commitment to growth and to building healthy, positive relationships with their girls flourished. Respectful and meaningful connections were becoming the norm. Self-care became a natural part of life. Elizabeth found Steve's ability to consistently pause and calm himself influenced her to do the same. Truly they were working as a team! Steve and Elizabeth shared what they felt was most essential for them to stay true to this course they were on—*to sustain and grow their Dream:*

- **Pausing**—This was essential for both of them to create the positive change they wanted and live their Dream.
- **Self-care**—Taking care of themselves with intentional date nights, bike riding, coffee breaks, space for individual quiet time, etc., really helped both Steve and Elizabeth be calm and confident in their parenting.
- **Teamwork**—Focusing on being a "united front" with their daughters felt key to their continued success...and gave them good reason for more dates as they sought time together to talk through issues regarding their daughters.
- **Encouraging self-talk**—As they grew their ability to intentionally switch up their self-talk to reflect what was positive and affirming, they found it kept their attention on what they wanted. This rippled out to have a positive effect on everything they did.

Steve and Elizabeth were more often living their Dream: **"We take care of ourselves and feel content and confident as parents. We parent calmly and respectfully, feeling joyfully connected with our children. We parent as a**

**team—encouraging, accepting, and welcoming the inde-
pendence of our children. We have fun together!"**

Their focus on self-care and their support and encouragement of each other to keep their self-care accounts full had
them feeling far more calm and confident no matter how their
girls decided to behave. The respect for each other they'd
grown during our coaching was just the right kind of role modeling for their daughters and provided a calm and safe environ-
ment in which the girls could act up, test, question, grow, and
learn. Even though there were still constant challenges, both
Steve and Elizabeth felt stronger as a couple and as individuals.
This strength allowed them to move through the challenges
with calm connection leading the way—and confidence following close behind. I noticed their newfound sense of humor—
the lightness and joy they expressed. I heard their relaxed tone
of voice (and chuckles!) as they shared the latest Bathroom
War between their two older daughters, the stubborn refusal
of their youngest to clean up toys, the cooking-experiment-
meant-to-be-dinner that failed—so different from early in our
coaching when they were angry, anxious, or totally confused
as to what to do. They no longer felt overwhelmed despite
the tumultuous times of tots and teens ☺. Experiencing their
Dream as more of the daily norm had them welcoming the
inevitable conflict with curiosity rather than judgment, and with
a quieter, calmer approach that gave them time to respond in
relationship-building ways. They were truly enjoying and celebrating the growth of their daughters!

It's Your Turn!

Destiny in your life

Now it is time to reflect on how YOU are living your Dream—in small or big ways; daily or now and again. Think about how you are feeling, what has shifted for you since you began this process. Has your anxiety lifted and a calmer, steadier feeling taken over? Does the morning transition flow more positively? Are you feeling more connected to your children? Do you find you no longer sweat the small stuff? Are you feeling confident throughout your day? Maybe you are better rested, realize you've had many days in a row with no tantrums, or your kids seem to play well on their own far more often. Perhaps you feel more focused and in the moment, truly enjoying being with your children despite all the distractions awaiting your attention. It can be enlightening to reflect on what initially brought you to this process, and what is different for you now—we often can't see the growth as we are immersed in it.

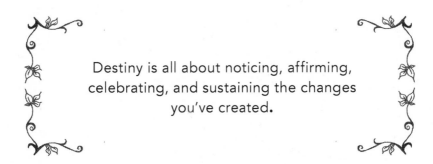

Destiny is all about noticing, affirming, celebrating, and sustaining the changes you've created.

Steps for continuing to grow and live your Dream:

1. **Ask yourself what action steps have helped you the most to sustain and grow your Dream**. Make a list and keep it short—name the steps or tools that have benefited you the most all along the way. Is it pause, self-care, clear frameworks, consistent follow-through, teamwork with your parenting partner? You know what has helped you the most.

2. **Ask yourself what these steps will require from you**, **what strengths of yours will need to step up.** Maybe it is your ability to be patient, to stay calm, to use pauses often. Maybe it is your proactive self planning ahead for babysitters in order to get the self-care you feel is most essential. Or maybe it is the compassion you show yourself as you move through tough moments or days with your child, sticking to the clear boundaries you've set no matter how difficult.

3. **Take time to reflect on what is reminding you of your Dream each day**. Notice the little things that are working and how you feel. When things go south (for they will!), think through a "do-over" as if your Dream was in place (what we focus on grows, so think it through based on how you'd like it to have gone, how you'd like to have felt). Be willing to tweak your Dream as life evolves. The more your "end" resonates with you, the more powerful and influential it can be, empowering you to persevere through challenging times.

4. **Look to what you can appreciate, what puts a smile on your face, no matter the chaos**. This is such an affirming thing to do! It can lighten things up and help you refocus on your Dream—empowering you to take the steps that will help you create the change you truly want.

5. **Keep "What you focus on grows" as your mantra and be sure to keep your focus on just what you want more of**!

6. **Keep self-care as a priority!** Little moments or long stretches of time. Deposit with intention often into your self-care account.

7. **Celebrate!** Take yourself out on a date, treat yourself to something special, toast yourself. It is essential to intentionally acknowledge your work and your success. This is the essence of self-care, of the foundation from which we can parent well. Go celebrate yourself!

A page for your reflections…

My story...

I have found incredible success in this Discover, Dream, Design, Destiny process in my own parenting journey, whether on a daily basis, a temporary basis, or long term. As my own daughters leave the nest to "fly" away as young women, I've experienced plenty of anxiety-driven periods during which I pause...breathe...and focus first on myself. I list what I can appreciate, what is working, what I see them doing well. I get clear on how I'd like things to unfold—and I write it up. A few examples include:

"My daughter embraces her new community with joy and ease. She connects with others genuinely, builds meaningful relationships, is energized by her work, and creates a life for herself that has her thriving."

My eldest moved out of the country to pursue graduate school—oh so difficult for us at home! Yes, we worried—she was so far away and in an unfamiliar place to us. By getting clear on what I hoped for her and putting it in writing, I found I calmed down and was more likely to interact with her based on how I'd feel if my Dream for her was in place—confident, relaxed, and curious. When she got caught in a struggle, she could hear my confidence in her, appreciate the questions I asked rather than the advice I could've given (and that was tough to do...withhold advice...), and fed off the relaxed energy I projected. What solid "deposits" into a healthy, positive relationship! The result? My eldest thrived in her new community, took charge of her life with energy and joy, met and enjoyed new people, and welcomed challenges and disappointment with a growing grace. It truly warmed my heart and put a smile on my face—and it still does, as I write this once again!

"My daughter lives strong and healthy, running with ease and strength. She knows just what she needs to thrive."

This Dream statement followed an injury that had my daughter unable to do the exercise she thrived on, feeling depressed, convinced that she'd never run again. It gave me a twinkle in my eye each time I read it, for I could picture her exactly as I stated it—running with ease and strength, ponytail flying behind her, strong legs carrying her far. And the energy, joy, and confidence I felt as I focused on this Dream directly influenced my interactions with her as she managed all parts of her medical care. I believe it communicated my confidence in her taking charge of her health, and allowed her to envision the light at the end of the tunnel she needed to be less immersed in the frustrations of her current reality. She felt empowered, and our relationship grew even stronger. The result? She was running the mountains she loved six months later. And thriving. Me? I was smiling!

"I intend to move through today fully present to my children, with plenty of time to do all that needs to be done, and feeling productive and peaceful throughout. We have fun today!"

Maybe you are starting the day stressed because it seems like it will be one of THOSE days. This statement is an example of how a Dream could look for a momentary situation or a day you think is headed south even before (or maybe as!) it does. For me, it is an affirmation of what I intend to have happen and how I want to feel right now, today, despite the expected chaos. By writing this and reflecting on it, I find I can "feel" the presence, the productiveness, and the peace. These feelings are real, for they are a part of successes I've already had and know that I want more of. I can tap into these feelings and take them into my busy day with my children. I can measure up the choices I make to my Dream statement, more likely creating just the kind of day I'd like—or at least, partially ☺. I find I may pause in my run down to switch laundry for the umpteenth time and consider if the peacefulness I intend to feel would be better achieved if I stopped for a moment to breathe, stretch, do something small just for me. I may hang up the phone sooner or just let it go to a message in order to give my full attention to my children (averting a potential meltdown and more likely enjoying a semblance of peace...). Perhaps it is calculating whether I'd feel more productive getting the floor vacuumed or the dirty dishes washed. If I get both done it would be a miracle!

The Dream I make at the start of my day empowers me to be more intentional with my choices, and I discover that my experience aligns itself with my statement. And if it still feels like chaos reigns? Then I intentionally look for the moments of my day that DID remind me of the Dream, even a little bit. Maybe it is the moment I put computer work aside and instead turned and really listened to my daughter. Maybe it was the pause I took to soak up a bit of sunshine on the back deck before tackling more of my chores, and the moment of peace it brought. Perhaps it was recognizing I got four of the six loads of wash started—maybe not finished, but started! I then can feel affirmed and encouraged...and maybe even think through what I could have done more of or differently to have even a better day. Now my attention is on just what I want more of (and as you now realize, what we focus on grows!) And my day ends up running more smoothly and my children and I have fun together. How cool is that?

I have trusted this process for a number of years and each time I am delighted and enriched. Slowly Appreciate Inquiry has become a way of life for me—nothing escapes my looking to what I want the most in a situation, to what is working, to what I can appreciate. And as a result, relationships have deepened and become more joyful; I feel clear, content, and confident much more often. I think you may be experiencing more of this, as well.

The process you've embraced in this book is more a practice to continue growing and strengthening, rather than a goal to achieve. Just as you reach a more centered and confident place, you can be sure life or children will bring you another round of chaos and challenge. And because you've been practicing and growing, you can enter into the next round stronger, more focused, able to parent from the "eye of the storm" rather than caught in the winds of chaos.

You will find the grace in the chaos, have more confidence in yourself, and experience the gentle joy that weaves itself all through your parenting journey. You will be parenting inspired! Inspired to grow, to create the kinds of relationships you want the most, to be your best. What a gift to your children, and to yourself.

Congratulations!

My best to you,

Alice

Acknowledgments

My work could only have been done because of the support I received from family, friends, and colleagues who read, reviewed, advised, designed, and ultimately inspired me. My gratitude goes to Rhonda Moskowitz, Joy Wilds, Theresa Perez, Michelle Hayworth, and Katrina Ryan for their support and guidance and active participation in my book; to my writing and publishing consultant, Anne Dubuisson, for her professional guidance throughout my entire writing process; to my husband, Mike, for generously giving me the space and time to write; to my daughter Emily for holding my hand (and teaching me new things!) through all the technology challenges I faced; and to my daughter Becky for her artistic endeavors as I worked to create a book that looked and felt like the treasure I intend it to be for all my readers.

I appreciate each of you and the many others who encouraged me through this process—with a special note of gratitude to Gloria DeGaetano of the Parent Coaching Institute and Hal Runkel of the ScreamFree Institute for being an integral part of my journey.

Thank you.

Alice Hanscam
PCI Certified Parent Coach® and Certified ScreamFree Leader

Endnotes

Introduction

[1] *Appreciative Inquiry: Change at the Speed of Imagination* by J. Watkins and B. Mohr, 2001. This resource (one of many) covers in depth the early timeline of AI's development and David Cooperrider's model for AI. More information can be found at the Appreciative Inquiry Commons: http://appreciativeinquiry.case.edu/

- A few other books modeling Appreciative Inquiry that have made a profound impact on me and the writing in this book include *Appreciative Living: The Principles of Appreciative Inquiry in Personal Life* by Jacqueline Kelm and *Dynamic Relationships: Unleashing the Power of Appreciative Inquiry in Daily Living* by Jacqueline Stavros and Cheri Torres. There are many more…

[2] David L. Cooperrider is the Fairmount Minerals Professor of Social Entrepreneurship at the Weatherhead School of Management, Case Western Reserve University. More information can be found at the Appreciative Inquiry Commons: http://appreciativeinquiry.case.edu/

[3] Visit www.thepci.org for more information on the Parent Coaching Institute and its founder, Gloria DeGaetano. My work through the PCI has been life changing for me—as a professional and as a parent.

[4] The "4 Ds" of Appreciative Inquiry is the process used for creating positive change. All of the above AI resources provide more in-depth coverage of them, as do other resources such as: http://en.wikipedia.org/wiki/Appreciative_inquiry.

[5] "What You/We Focus on Grows" is evolved from the Parent Coaching Institute's Living System Principles™, a part of the Parent

Coach Certification® Training Program created by Gloria DeGaetano. Visit www.thepci.org for more information.

[6] Pausing is a foundational piece to Hal Runkel's *ScreamFree Parenting: The Revolutionary Approach to Rising Your Kids by Keeping Your Cool.* The Power of Pause phrase evolved through work with other PCI Certified Parent Coaches® and the ScreamFree Institute, www.screamfree.com.

[7] The concept of self-care as a foundational piece of parenting and living well comes from many sources, as well as personal experience. *Take Time for Your Life* by Cheryl Richardson, *ScreamFree Parenting* by Hal Runkel, and the Parent Coach Certification® Training Program created by Gloria DeGaetano for the Parent Coaching Institute have influenced me the most. There are many, many other resources showing the essential nature of caring first for ourselves.

[8] The emphasis on focusing first on yourself was greatly influenced by both the Parent Coaching Institute's Living System Principles™ and *ScreamFree Parenting* by Hal Runkel.

Dream

[1] "Thoughtful wishing" was brought to my attention in *ScreamFree Parenting*, by Hal Runkel. He refers to it alongside his principle of "Begin with the end in mind, but let go of the final results" as a response from C. S. Lewis "urging (his) readers to concentrate on their deepest longings for the future." (*ScreamFree Parenting*, 68)

[2] "End in mind" is evolved from "Begin with the End in Mind" found in *7 Habits of Highly Effective Families* by Stephen Covey.

[3] The Miracle Day was evolved from "The Miracle Question," first developed by Steve de Shazer and Insoo Kim Berg in their Solution Focused Brief Therapy work. It is used in varying forms by many in the social work, coaching, and therapy world.

[4] Adapted from "Imagine Your Child as an Adult," written by Gloria DeGaetano for the Parent Coach Certification® Training Program. www.ParentCoachInternational.com. Used with permission.

[5] "Begin with the End in Mind" originates from *7 Habits of Highly Effective People and 7 Habits of Highly Effective Families*, both by Stephen Covey. I use it with permission from the FranklinCovey Company.

[6] Evolved by Hal Runkel (*ScreamFree Parenting*) from Stephen Covey's original "Begin with the End in Mind." Used with permission.

[7] From *Appreciative Living: The Principles of Appreciative Inquiry in Personal Life* (by Jacqeuline Kelm, 79) in reference to Margaret Wheatley's metaphor for vision in *Leadership and the New Science*.

Design

[1] "Keep your promises" comes from *ScreamFree Parenting*, by Hal Runkel

Made in the USA
Lexington, KY
25 January 2016